JAMES MONT

The King Cole Penthouse

JAMES MONT

The King Cole Penthouse

by Todd Merrill

TODD MERRILL & ASSOCIATES, INC.
NEW YORK

This catalog was published on the occassion of the exhibition James Mont: The King Cole Penthouse, held at Todd Merrill Exhibition Space, 63-65 Bleecker Street, New York, NY 10012 from October 15, 2007 to December 2007.

Copyright © 2007 Todd Merrill & Associates, Inc., New York
All rights reserved under the international and Pan-American copyright conventions

ISBN 978-0-6151-7996-4

With contributions by
Roberta Maneker for Todd Merrill & Associates, Inc.
Erin Johnson for Todd Merrill & Associates, Inc.

All images in the book are the copyright of Todd Merrill & Associates, Inc. unless otherwise specified.

Front cover: Detail Image of Monumental Chest of Drawers
    by James Mont, 1963

Photography: Joe Cernius for Todd Merrill & Associates, Inc.

Frontispiece: Character drawing of James Mont by James Mont

Distributed worldwide by LuLu.com on-line publishing

Designed by William Indursky of FLASHcap Interactive
Printed and bound by LuLu.com on-line publishing

Printed in The United States of America

CONTENTS

Foreword	7
Acknowledgments	9
Introduction To James Mont	12
The Orlowitz Collection from the King Cole Penthouse, Miami Beach	20
Exhibition & Sale Catalog	28
Dining Room	31
Living Room	39
Master Bedroom	55
Chinoiserie Bar	67
Selection of Other James Mont Items	79
Index	104
Concept Drawings	
Selected Bibliography	109

FOREWORD

In the spring of 2000, I opened a small antique shop on the Lower Eastside of Manhattan specializing in vintage modern furniture and period antiques. Very quickly my attention turned from my lifelong passion for period American furniture to the new and fascinating area of post WWII furniture and the artisans who made it. I found the designers to be distinctly American, expressing a wide range of aesthetic styles, from the experimental handcrafted organic wood pieces to the high glam furniture of James Mont.

Bill Moore, one of the best pickers of vintage modern furniture who began his career in the mid 1990s working at the pioneering modern shop 280 Modern, introduced me to James Mont. Shortly after I opened at 100 Stanton Street he brought me an oversized pair of gilded Buddha lamps, circa 1950. I had never seen anything like them. The overall dramatic effect was incredible and the detail, especially the patinated gilded finish, was of a quality I had only seen on the finest period furniture. They consisted of a pair of "found objects"—large pottery Thai Buddha—mounted on carved block bases and fitted with oversized shades. The brass metal leaf finish was thinly applied over a multi-layered base of subtle colors and then patinated with acids to achieve an antique bronze effect. The shades were decorated with applied molded plaster that were carved, gilded and patinated to match the base and jumbo gilded wooden tassels fit for a harem hung as the pull switches. Theatrical, oversized and glowing with gold and bronze, these Buddha were staged to stop you in your tracks. What a pair of lamps, I thought! Almost tacky, but not—really sophisticated and chic—a bit on the edge and truly glamorous.

Who was this James Mont? I would soon discover through my acquisitions that he was a larger-than-life, complex American character of Turkish descent whose life is worthy of a movie and whose creative vision was totally original.

Those lamps sold immediately to Kelly Wearstler of KWID in Los Angeles, for her own home, one of the first decorators to really understand and use Mont's aesthetic. I began to buy every piece I could find. Often the pieces were as odd as they were beautiful and well made.

Over the years as my business grew, my interest in Mont gradually approached obsession. In 2006, I moved my shop to the Louis Sullivan building at 65 Bleecker Street and eventually my inventory multiplied into the thousands. At the same time, I emptied my Chelsea apartment of all the 18th and 19th century furnishings (literally my grandparent's) and began to live with the designers I was selling.

One of my first major Mont pieces was a large Chinoiserie console. I could not figure this piece out. It looked a bit like Moderne from the 1930s, but was made in the late 1950s for a Sutton Place apartment. It was finished with layer upon layer of Cinnabar colored lacquer, rubbed to reveal the layers beneath to give a faded effect. A Chinese screen was gilded to perfection and staged against smoked-black mirror at the center of the console. The proportions were lost in my cavernous shop but when moved to my apartment it was perfection. I began to live with James Mont designs. Soon nearly everything in my living room was Mont.

In early 2007, I received an invitation to go to Miami and see what was described to me as "the

FOREWORD

last great apartment designed by James Mont" in the once extremely glamorous and moneyed King Cole Apartments. The original owner's daughter sold the apartment intact to Dr. Judith Berson-Levinson. She and her husband lived in what was practically a 40 year old Mont museum. They were selling the apartment and all the original furnishings and fixtures. I arrived with my former assistant, David Sullivan, to photograph the apartment and to purchase the furniture. Upon arrival the entrance and interior were overwhelming, both in the theatrical effect and in the combination of Classical and Chinese design elements. We were looking at the decor through nearly 40 years of wear and resurfacing, but it was all still there. David's immediate reaction was, "you cannot do this, man." But like a good mentor I made him sit down and take it all in—"look at it until you get it."

It was apparent that Mont was given carte blanche to create a dramatic and luxurious interior in what once was the finest piece of ocean front property in Miami Beach. I could hear the Rat Pack singing and see the influence of Hollywood movies from the white painted and gilded classical columns, which immediately reminded me of the set of Elizabeth Taylor's Cleopatra, to the dark and smoky Asian bar. This was a fantasy interior like no other—I was finally beginning to understand James Mont.

Dr. Berson-Levinson acquired not only most of the original furnishings but also many of Mont's concept drawings, blueprints, correspondence and invoices. It was a fully documented time capsule and treasure trove. The pieces were a bit tattered and over-painted, but the vision and ingenuity was still there. It was irresistible to me—I had to have it and return it to its original glamour and beauty.

I purchased nearly every piece of furniture from Mont's original design and began a painstaking process to restore each to its original surface. In the process of researching this collection I met Sheri Orlowitz, daughter of Ellis, who grew up in the apartment. She kept the few missing pieces and documents in storage for 25 years. After purchasing these I was able to reunite the entire collection.

The Orlowitz Collection shows James Mont at the pinnacle of his career. With decades of experience behind him this would be his last great fully executed custom interior. While most designers in the 1960s experimented with new materials and outrageous forms, Mont continued to design with reverence for the past and to perfect his "Chinese Modern" style, a term he coined. The end result is a collaboration between myself and James Mont – a collection glowing in silver and gold leaf, black lacquer and smoked mirror. It is at once brazenly dramatic yet softened by time and Mont's numerous references to past civilizations and old Hollywood glamour.

Todd Merrill
October 2007

ACKNOWLEDGMENTS

This book and catalogue has been possible with the help of my staff at Todd Merrill & Associates: Gabrielle Auerbach, David Carpenter, Joe Cernius, Erin Johnson, Troy Seidman, Bruno Ryan Kozar and former employees and friends David Sullivan and Jennifer Kaplan. Thank you to my steadfast movers John Marin, Fernando Munoz and Juan Hernandez.

Special thanks to my webmaster and graphic designer Bill Indursky and his partner David Ryskiewich for their untiring work and support.

Many thanks to my former boss at Christie's Roberta Maneker, who has been kind enough to write for this project in her spare time. My publicist Christina Juarez, cabinet maker Eric Chapeau and upholsterer Angel Puma.

Thanks for the generous support, information and photos from Sheri Orlowitz, Dr. Judi Berson-Levinson and Steven Z. Levinson, Gerald Friedland, John Sollo of Sollo/Rago Auctions and the librarians at the Cooper-Hewitt National Design Museum and the Smithsonian Institution.

Lastly, Thank you to my parents and grandparents for raising me in this wonderful business and for teaching me the basics and allowing me to always grow and learn. And for her enduring support and devotion my wife Lauren Merrill.

ESSAYS

Archive Image 1
James Mont (right) with Sophie Tucker (left) signed by Sophie Tucker, ca 1950.

INTRODUCTION TO JAMES MONT

Archive Image 2
Picture of James Mont (middle) with Best Man Bob Hope (left) and new bride Helen Kim (right).

Roué, rogue and man–about–town, James Mont (1904-1978) was a charismatic charmer with high-profile clients and an anger management problem. Along the way – and his way was wayward – he is said to have designed interiors for show business marquee names such as Bob Hope (best man at Mont's wedding), Irving Berlin and Lana Turner. More firmly documented is the work he did for east-coast Mafiosi, including Frank Costello and Lucky Luciano, which likely began during Prohibition when Mont created unique custom bars for their homes. Hot-headed and mercurial, Mont's bad temper and willfulness got him in trouble and debt repeatedly during a roller-coaster career lasting four decades. As a designer, his creativity, perfectionism and delight in innovation produced both elegant, high style interiors and over-the-top kitsch.

Demetrios Pecintoglu – aka James Mont and James Pess – was born in Istanbul, the son of a noted sculptor-designer. After studying art and architecture in Spain and France, in 1922 he emigrated to the United States and soon had a shop in Atlantic City New Jersey, and friendships with the big boys. By 1932 Mont had a flourishing design business and a well-located shop in midtown Manhattan which probably was bankrolled by his shady pals. As a businessman he was volatile and impulsive, unstable in many ways. Over the years, his leases changed hands with the speed of a Three-card Monte dealer as he nimbly dodged bill- and tax-collectors, often successfully but going bankrupt three times (in 1934, 1946 as James Pess, and 1952).

Mustached and balding, more suave than handsome, Mont enjoyed the notoriety of celebrities and gangsters, and the kicks of fashionable nightclubs, booze and bimbos. His

INTRODUCTION TO JAMES MONT

salacious personal life was anchored oh-so-briefly by a marriage, in 1937, to a 25-year-old Korean-American stage actress named Helen Kim who committed suicide in their Park Avenue apartment 29 days after their wedding, landing Mont on the front pages of New York's newspapers. Not for the last time. He sat out World War II in a Sing Sing cell, sentenced to five-to-ten years for assaulting a female business associate who thereafter killed herself.

But loosey-goosey as he was in his personal life, he was generous with friends and strangers and he was serious when it came to his work. Spotting a need – call it a social need – soon after immigrating during the Prohibition 1920s, he began designing custom bars – not only for thugs, but for homes and businesses. From this early success, Mont built a business designing a broad line of home furnishings, although his association with these bars, some of them remarkably clever, lasted through most of his career. Mont held patents on two designs – a decorative service bar (1937) and a collapsible, fold-up home bar (as late as 1953).

As a custom designer, his taste always ran to opulence and drama, and a typical Mont interior was filled with frequently big and usually comfortable pieces. In a 1934 Art Digest article, Mont stated that "today, the keynote of modern furniture is in its simplicity. Modern design has not reached the last word, but then art is not interested in last words. The modern furniture of today expresses our particular form of style, pleasure and comfort." Much of his pre-World War II work leaned toward too-muchness but over the years he

Archive Image 3
James Mont promotional photo of Collapsible Bar design, ca 1937.

Archive Image 4
James Mont promotional photo of Collapsible Bar design, ca 1937.

INTRODUCTION TO JAMES MONT

Archive Image 5
Headshot from James Mont's promotional pamphlet "Mont Moods", ca 1950.

refined his sensibilities somewhat, and his later work is characterized by a strong Asian flavor. Never accused of subtlety, he nonetheless was able to produce dramatic interiors of elegance and high style, frequently managing to stay just this side of excess.

He was partial to exotic Oriental motifs, perhaps the influence of his natal land, and is closely identified with "Chinese modern," a term he claimed to have coined. Mitchell Owens in the New York Times (April 4, 1996) described Mont's work as "a stylish uptown fusion of Eastern silhouettes and Western modernism." Owens later described his style as "a look that could be called Runyon Moderne, beefy, broad-shouldered objects imbued with a Pacific Rim flavor that appealed to gun molls and their brass-knuckled protectors."

When Mont was on his game, he produced custom pieces on a grand scale that flashed a distinctive Hollywood glamour and a hint of the mysteries of the Orient —mirrors, faux animal skins, vivid colors, and plenty of silver and gilt. Pieces were large, sleek, exquisitely crafted and often fabulous. He was equally capable of unrestrained and flamboyant designs that were more grandiose than grand.

Many Mont pieces are distinguished by wonderfully sumptuous surface textures – luscious finishes which included distressed, wormy and limed woods, layers of silver and gold leaf, and lustrous, deeply lacquered pieces – 14 or 15 hand polished layers were typical. A New York Times article (July 1, 1945) describes one of Mont's technique for adding texture to wood: "the wood is grooved by sandblasting, then treated with stale beer and rottenstone...." and, finally, given a pickled finish. Mont said that he learned many of

INTRODUCTION TO JAMES MONT

his techniques through extended experimentation during his years in prison.

Given the labor-intensive and time-consuming processes involved in making his one-off pieces, it is not surprising that his work was expensive for its time. But his craftsmanship and attention to detail were unsurpassed. Mont had the zeal of a perfectionist. He was genuinely finicky about his work, but also theatrical to the core, known to occasionally destroy a piece with (or without) a slight imperfection, to demonstrate his extraordinarily high standards to a stunned client who might immediately sign on the dotted line. According to the son of Mont's long-time lawyer David Friedland, if he didn't like a customer, he threw him out. And Mont was tyrannical – you took what he wanted you to take.

Mont operated out of a number of facilities in the course of his career. The man was peripatetic (remember those bill-collectors) and over the years had various shops in New Jersey, Long Island, Miami Beach, and even Greece. His first big-time Manhattan location was on Fifth Avenue (1932), reputedly underwritten by his loyal gangster clients. This was followed by 37 West 57th St. where he did business as Maison Decors, Inc. (1937), 548 Madison Avenue at the corner of 55th St. (1938), and 310 East 59th St. Much of Mont's best work was created in the years right after the war and his release from prison, when under the name Modern Mode he produced sleek and sophisticated pieces from a five-story building at 214-216 East 52nd Street, employing some 50 workers. Friedland says each floor housed a different stage of

Archive Image 6
Headshot from James Mont's promotional pamphlet "Mont Moods", ca 1950.

Archive Image 7
James Mont's "Chinese Modern" booth at the 1939 New York World's Fair.

INTRODUCTION TO JAMES MONT

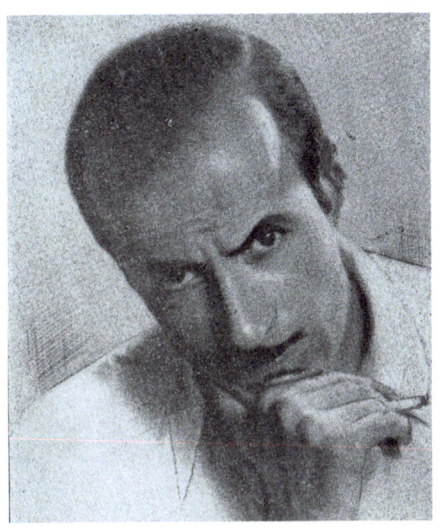

Archive Image 8
Headshot from James Mont's promotional pamphlet "Mont Moods", ca 1950.

manufacture, the showroom at ground level, leather workers on one floor, lacquerers on another, and so on. Friedland says Mont claimed to be the first designer to set up his showroom as individual room tableaux.

In 1952, Mont was in deep financial trouble again. His inventory and his personal collection of Oriental arts were sold at a forced two-part public liquidation sale at Savoy Galleries. He rebounded, of course, but by the 1960s the parade was passing him by. Nonetheless he snagged a large commission in Miami Beach – a 3,000+ square foot penthouse on Bay Drive in a fancy building called the King Cole, and although most of Mont's custom interiors went unphotographed, this showcase apartment was the exception. The home is archetypal Mont. The classical Greek mise-en-scène is established on the outside of the front door with a massive medallion-studded cream and gold pediment and fluted columns flanking marble niches and a black paneled and lacquered door. A Greek key theme undulates through the entire apartment, decorating every conceivable surface, from the lacquered black baby grand piano to table aprons, chair arms and closet drawers. Greek columns are incorporated in the living room design. The "entertainment room" escaped – it is Asian themed, paneled and lacquered in orange and black – in contrast to the rich Roman style in most of the other rooms – with recessed orange niches holding Oriental objets d'art. Aside: during this period he was said to have built an Orientalized house boat on Indian Creek where he lived with one of his girlfriends.

Mont didn't limit himself to big jobs. A small-scale project was featured in a New York Times article on "Space-saving Devices to Expand a Tiny Apartment," wherein he utilized build-in cabinets,

INTRODUCTION TO JAMES MONT

shelves to replace tables, and sofas that serve as beds. (Friedland reports that it actually was Mont's apartment.) And, deploying profound self-confidence and a quirky imagination, he could respond to challenges by producing innovative and problem-solving pieces. For example, he designed a table that converted to a 10-foot-long library ladder, and a coffee table with optional secret compartments. He claimed credit for having invented the sofa bed, and did in fact patent a sofa design in 1947.

Ever the showman, Mont was a facile and playful marketer. One example is the goofy self-promotional book he wrote, "The Young Physician's Road Map," illustrated with clever cartoons showing Mont as he was – gambler, boozer, ladies' man – all to promote an inventory sale prior to doubling his space at the 214 East 52nd St. premises. He described another Mont-penned pamphlet, "All Gall is Divided into Three Parts," as an "amusing and instructive booklet on interior decoration."

Actually, it was Mont who had many parts, including gall. Extravagant, hot-tempered, theatrical, generous, egotistical, even dangerous – he was not your typical genteel designer. He was an original.

Essay By Roberta Maneker for Todd Merrill & Associates, Inc.

Archive Images 9 - 12
Page from James Mont's promotional pamphlet "The Young Physician's Roadmap," ca 1950.

INTRODUCTION TO JAMES MONT

THE YOUNG PHYSICIAN'S ROADMAP

BY

JAMES MONT,

D.I.D.

Let's start off by admitting you're sick. You must be, or you wouldn't be getting a copy of this; our mailing list is stolen from the Mayo clinic.

You've been a little tense lately. When you unwind, there's a zinging noise, like a cheap Swiss watch crossing the border. You're so out of sorts, a singing commercial for Serutan sounds good to your ears and it seems the announcer is talking directly to you when he describes what Lydia Pinkham's Compound is good for.

He said I ought to get away from it all . . . take a vacation under the Florida sun. I'd come back feeling fit as a fuddle.

Well, you know how that turned out. The closest I got to a palm tree was the plaster-of-Paris kind they had in the bar of the Saxony Hotel. I swam a good deal, but only going through doors. Before I went away, any loud noise would make my nerves jangle like a doorbell. When I got back, they twitched every time my cat crossed his legs.

He told me to take up therapy in Miami, so I went out to Hialeah race track for a little basket weaving.

One day was enough to make my spirits lighter, exactly $1,406 lighter.

I came home feeling tanned as an old shoe and just as peppy.

For a while, I took some home remedies. A client told me that one of the best things I could do was relax with half a pint of Scotch just

A psychiatrist would charge you money to advise you to weave baskets as a hobby. And he doesn't tell you what to do with the baskets (if he's a gentleman).

We'll diagnose your case, write the prescription, give you all the instructions you need and furnish the materials. When you're through, you'll have new beauty added to your home and, most important, your bank balance will not have come down with an acute case of anemia.

Of course, if a needle makes you nervous, you can brush right by our upholstery, our fabrics and our frames departments—straight to the finished products on our showroom floors. They're also marked a whacking 50% off for this "Bare Bones" alteration sale. Believe us, you'll never have a better opportunity to give your home a rejuvenation treatment at clinic prices.

This will be the last time this year Modern Mode Furniture Company will offer any of our "Originals for 1950" below list price, so we hope you'll take advantage of this sale.

As for our custom decorator service, we're sorry to advise we've just about closed the books for this year. If you've been planning on a complete interior decorating of your home in the near future, we'd be delighted to get together with you, however, just so the date is some time in 1951. For a limited number of our customers, we'll even start the initial step of that dream home, by producing your own individual plan, from architectural blue prints right down to samples of wallpaper. You'll find details of this plan on the inside back cover of this booklet.

So please pay us a visit . . . . . . the sooner the better, if you're the sturdy builder type. If you only want to find out how a chair is put together, you're still welcome. And it's information that might come in handy; maybe you'll be a pioneer before you're through.

We'll be looking to see you, today, at Modern Mode's

BARE BONES SALE
50% off
As ever,
JAMES MONT, D. I. D.

complete interior decorating plan for
your apartment or "town house" . . .

This is what you get: blueprint plan for from one to three rooms, in scale and detailing all furniture arrangement. Color schemes for walls, woodwork, carpets, furniture, draperies and fabrics with material swatches and wallpaper samples included. All for $100.

Note: Should you engage James Mont to carry out the decorator plans outlined above, the cost of the plans will be deducted from the total price of your contract.

MODERN MODE FURNITURE CO., INC.
214 EAST 52ND STREET, NEW YORK, N. Y.
EL 5-6735

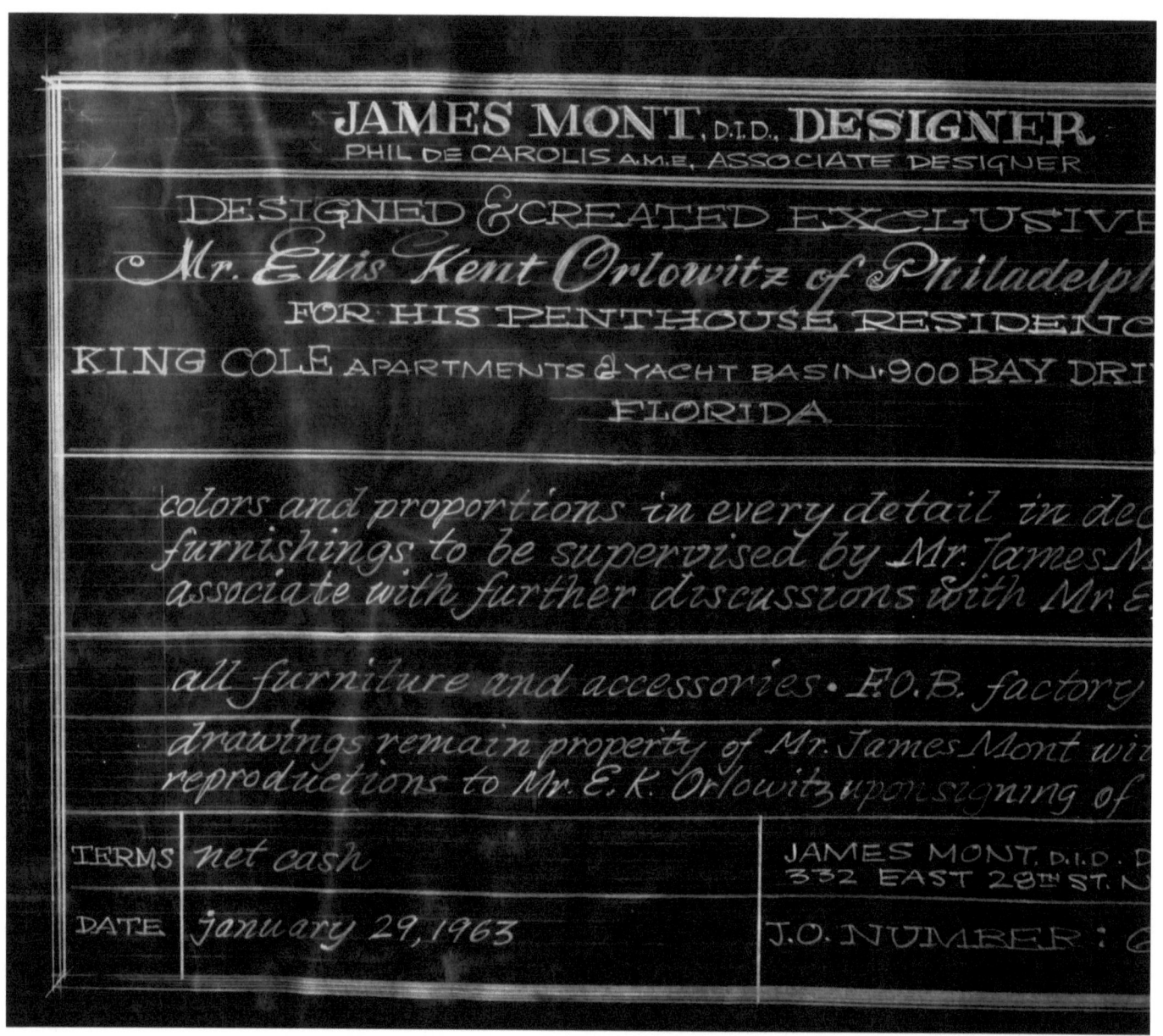

Dwg. 1
Titleblock and "contract for work" for Orlowitz King Cole Penthouse by James Mont, ca. 1963.

THE ORLOWITZ COLLECTION
FROM THE KING COLE PENTHOUSE
MIAMI BEACH

James Mont was known for his extreme temper tantrums, his questionable clientele, his frequent abscondence and his internationally eclectic furniture. Seldom discussed are his penchant for pretty ladies and his generosity—these contrary traits undoubtedly materialized in his furniture and interiors. The Orlowitz Collection exemplifies James Mont's imaginative, exotic designs and capricious behavior.

Using strong colors and eclectic forms, Mont created fantastic interiors indicative of a Eurasian harem or the 1930s El Morocco nightclub in New York City. Pomp and flare, glitz and glamour, dark and dramatic best describe Mont's design of Ellis Orlowitz's Miami penthouse. The apartment, a tour de force in Greek and Asian motifs, was one of Mont's last commissions before he retired. A total work of art was produced with attention to every detail, typical of Mont's work.

Todd Merrill Antiques is proud to exhibit this collection of James Mont furniture. This is the first comprehensive exhibition in the United States on the elusive designer that features a James Mont interior intact from a single owner collection and demonstrates Mont at his best. It is also the first fully documented collection with contracts, correspondence, concept drawings and a floor plan. Ellis Orlowitz, a long time friend and patron of James Mont, had two other Mont designed homes— and as such Mont was given carte blanche in 1963 to create an entire home in upscale Miami Beach at the posh King Cole Apartments. From doorknobs, cornices, carpets and state beds, everything in the Orlowitz penthouse represents Mont's ability to design whole interiors.

Even though clients knew to relinquish control and trust Mont's vision, many stories expose Mont's crazed behavior when clients and workmen didn't acquiesce. Perhaps his temper tantrums were the result of the copious amounts of coffee he drank, as Ms. June Greenfield—Ellis Orlowitz's first wife —remembers when she met Mont back in 1945. She remembers him as "unusual, gregarious, and talkative," and explains her home in Philadelphia, PA that Mont designed felt like "living in a nightclub." She also recollects bizarre moments when Mont unexpectedly and fanatically jumped up and down on his furniture for no apparent reason. From throwing furniture down stairs to yelling at clients, his passion for his work was immeasurable. Regardless of the melodrama, his animated and electric personality drew people to him; and not just anyone, his pieces were expensive and his clientele was willing to pay. His clients ranged from the Mafioso to Hollywood celebrities to people who just had to live with all things "Montish".

James Mont was a purveyor of taste in all things international and was emphatic about quality. The Turkish born designer incorporated found objects from Asia or embellished Greek motifs in his furniture. And his obsession to gild and lacquer pieces to perfection produced a unique, original look that is difficult to replicate. In Mont's 5-story workshop on East 52nd street an entire floor was dedicated to gilding and lacquering. As a student of art and architecture in Spain and France, then as an apprentice in a Parisian furniture manufacture, Mont was extremely well versed in fine craftsmanship and furniture production, and therefore hired the finest craftsmen but oversaw all levels of production. His perfectionism, however,

THE ORLOWITZ COLLECTION
FROM THE KING COLE PENTHOUSE
MIAMI BEACH

led to an intolerable behavior when things were not to his specifications.

The gilding process was the most labor intensive at his workshop. Mont's technique used several layers of primer in varying colors to obtain the perfect undertone to his gilding. Depending on his desired look, he usually started with a base coat of stone gray then added a combination of thin layers—sometimes upwards of fifteen—ranging from lavender and pale green to rose and light blue or charcoal black. His camouflage technique involved both silver and gold leaf and he wanted the under color to resonate differently under each gilded leaf, but to simultaneously harmonize in pattern and hue throughout the surface. Occasionally, his smoky lacquer technique was added by brushing over the leaf with a light charcoal color mixed with the lacquer, which added a hazed patina effect. This technique involved applying thick coats of smoked lacquer then gently rubbing it off leaving certain areas darker than others but keeping the haze throughout. After adding a thin sheath of silver or gold leaf and heavy lacquer, the final result was a luminous surface with a hint of color permeating through. Once Mont's technique is understood, his demanding and erratic personality starts to make sense.

Most designers in the early 1960s strove for fresh new forms and ambiguity in their designs, which opposed the stark adherence to the rules of standardization of the 1950s. While mainstream designers separated from the International Style and ventured into flexible and synthetic furniture, Mont stayed true to his ubiquitous Greco-Roman Chinese modern designs and traditional materials.

Asian Figural Lamp
An Asian figure carved in driftwood with multi-layered hand rubbed gilded finish in tones of pale blue, gray and variegated gold. Original hand painted and gilded parchment shade.

Console
Features two cabinets with doors and one center false cabinet, doors mounted with pierced, carved and gilded square pulls, all on a platform base, finished in gold on silver leaf camouflage pattern. Shown on the original furnished floor plan by James Mont and listed on Mont's Contract Specifications.

THE ORLOWITZ COLLECTION
FROM THE KING COLE PENTHOUSE
MIAMI BEACH

Dwg. 4
Elevation drawing of front entrance of Orlowitz King Cole Penthouse by James Mont, ca 1963.

Archive Image 13
Front entrance of Orlowitz King Cole Penthouse, photo by Sheri Orlowitz ca 1970, photo courtesy Sheri Orlowitz.

He, too, wanted the beauty and utility technology offered, but his heritage and personality guided him, not technology and theories. His heritage was rich with history and elegance, and he undoubtedly got inspiration from such magnificent examples as the Topkapi Palace in Istanbul, Turkey. This palace is known for its extravagant warren of rooms, its asymmetrical layout and Ottoman style architecture. This essay gives a virtual tour of the 1963 James Mont designed King Cole penthouse and shows that Mont was a glitzy, international iconoclast in a field of theorizing conformists.

The entrance to Ellis Orlowitz's apartment prepared visitors for the theatrical interior they were about to experience: A pediment in cream and gold, flanked by Corinthian columns framed a recessed black lacquered door embellished with two square gilded doorknobs with Asian symbol motifs. Once inside, the Asian infused Greek inspired wonderment of color and texture was abound; the entire penthouse appeared to be a scene from Joseph Mankiewicz's 1963 movie Cleopatra. Mont repeated motifs throughout the penthouse to unify the spaces: Greek and Chinese key motifs, Corinthian and Doric columns, pagoda pediments, emblems of swans, lions, swags, urns, and Venuses all gilded to perfection.

The foyer had a metal skylight trickling light onto the warm yellow walls that blended perfectly with the gilded molding on the door. A pared down Ionic entablature framed a door that was inset with a large sandblasted glass panel incised with a Grecian urn, stylized swags and sinewy flowers. And the white marble floor had a black border that mirrored the molding on the door.

Guests then ventured into the equally opulent, spacious living room that featured large fluted

THE ORLOWITZ COLLECTION
FROM THE KING COLE PENTHOUSE
MIAMI BEACH

columns and silver gilt and black lacquered furniture that fit the room's proportion. A chair rail adorned with Chinese fretwork molding was a specific meander that repeated throughout the home. Moldings shaped as cartouches lined each wall, rectangular cartouches below the chair rail and elongated octagonal cartouches above. The gilded, crenellated crown molding matched the molding on the black baby grand piano that anchored the room.

Opposite the elegant piano, Mont's concept drawings specified a seating area with two sofas, end tables and a console surrounding one large cocktail table to balance the room. The cocktail table's base is a bronze Corinthian capital whose former home was atop a column located on a Manhattan bank building. Mont gilded the base and designed a round top with a Chinese fretwork decorating its apron. The ensemble fit within an island of orange shag carpet surrounded by a marble floor.

Situated adjacent to the piano were large black and gold chairs and a side table similar to the cocktail table but Mont employed a Romanesque form for the pedestal base. The entire room, with the chair arm supports in an open Greek key form, the table tops with Chinese fretwork borders, and the classically formed pedestal bases, hearkened back to a Roman palace interior with a Chinese flare.

Visible from the living room was the dining room's back wall that featured a door-surround treated with classical elements: fluted pilasters, pedestals and entablature. The door-surround had a niche that housed a

Dwg. 9
Perspective drawing of living room of Orlowitz King Cole Penthouse by James Mont, ca 1963.

Documentary Photo 5
Vintage photo of the back foyer from The Orlowitz King Cole Penthouse by James Mont, ca 1963.

THE ORLOWITZ COLLECTION
FROM THE KING COLE PENTHOUSE
MIAMI BEACH

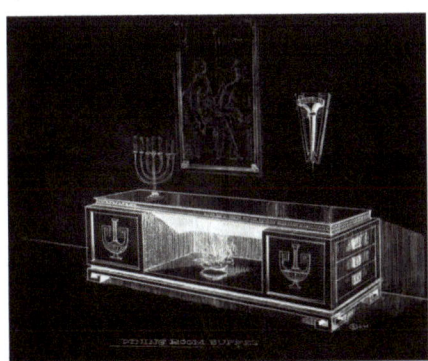

Dwg. 7
Perspective drawing of dining room buffet of Orlowitz King Cole Penthouse by James Mont, ca 1963.

Dining Console
Top inset with smoked-mirror panel into a gold metal leaf frame with Chinoiserie fretwork carved edge, mounted on top of an antiqued silver leaf cabinet inset with two smoked-mirror panels, each panel with carved Classical urn gold metal leaf appliqué, three mirrored drawers on each end of the sideboard that rests on a Greek key base.

bronze statue of a woman. Placed on either side of the faux doorway were giant bronze jardinière sconces in the shape of an acanthus leaf and each had a large topiary sprouting up the wall. One sidewall was lined with five arch-shaped cartouche panels accentuated with gilded gadroon molding, and painted in each panel was a gold elongated scepter-like figure.

The sole embellishment on the opposite wall was the large gilded and mirrored sideboard and a painting of Ellis Orlowitz's choice. Carved Chinese fretwork borders the top edge of the gilded sideboard. The piece consists of three compartments, the center compartment without doors. Applied to each outer compartment is a stylized Grecian urn. On both ends of the sideboard are three drawers with square pulls with an Asian symbol form. The sideboard rests on a platform raised by open Greek key formed feet. The same key formed feet supports the dining table's fluted column pedestal base. The table and chairs have Chinese fretwork carved aprons, and the chairs' back splats are an elongated Greek key form that completes the ensemble.

Mont's original proposal used two dining room tables rather than one large one. Also, Mont did not produce a bar cart in the form of a Roman chariot, complete with a horse head, horsewhip and space for drinking accoutrements; an addition that would've delighted Orlowitz's guests as they dined.

The bar room was the only room decorated in a Chinese theme. Three walls were covered in textured plaster then painted gold. Every space in the bar room was dedicated to Chinese antiques: porcelain, statues, cinnabar vessels and 19th century woodcuts. Iconic 1960s orange shag

THE ORLOWITZ COLLECTION
FROM THE KING COLE PENTHOUSE
MIAMI BEACH

carpeting complemented the equally iconic stalactite plaster ceiling. The bar was set against a background of a gray wood paneled wall with niches for barware and various Chinese sculptures. Its top was black and heavily lacquered and the front had orange stained panels, each inset with a giant gilded Chinese symbol. The niches, two horizontal and four vertical, were framed in gilded wood and placed on either side of a cinnabar stained door.

Pagoda shaped pediments accentuated the doorframe and vertical niches. The ceiling above the bar was lowered, stained a burnt orange and adorned with gilded Chinese symbols. Complemented by low furniture in a gilded finish, Mont's design created a charming and inviting atmosphere. The one armed "opium den" sofa opposite the bar sat on a long gilded platform that ended with a built in side table. A low gilded coffee table and black lacquered, gold trimmed pagoda cabinet sat adjacent to the sofa and both displayed various Asian antiques.

Ellis Orlowitz spared no expense for Mont to create a grandiose bedroom fit for a king. With its own private entrance, large-scale furnishings and hidden compartments it was grand and luxurious. The foyer had exposed aggregate walls and gilded sconces that gave a faint glow, when combined with the camouflage gilt and heavily lacquered console. The result was a warm and sultry invitation to the small entranceway.

Once inside the bedroom, Mont's typical Greco-Roman themes continued with the dramatic dark and heavily gilded treatment. Walls with gilded Greek key crown molding, floor-to-ceiling windows and large Doric columns surrounded the inhabitants. At the right of the entrance was a silver leaf desk with a double pedestal base, each adorned with a lion's head roundel and a Greek Key border around the top.

Dwg. 13
Perspective drawing of Chinoisiere Bar of Orlowitz King Cole Penthouse by James Mont, ca.1963.

Documentary Photo 7
Vintage photo of the Chinoisiere Bar from The Orlowitz King Cole Penthouse by James Mont, ca 1963.

THE ORLOWITZ COLLECTION
FROM THE KING COLE PENTHOUSE
MIAMI BEACH

Dwg. 10
Perspective drawing of bed in the Master Bedroom of Orlowitz King Cole Penthouse by James Mont, ca 1963.

Dwg. 11
Perspective drawing of bedroom chest of Orlowitz King Cole Penthouse by James Mont, ca.1963.

A silver and gilt camouflaged klimos chair complemented the desk. But the impressive state bed and cabinets overshadowed the diminutive desk.

From Mont's concept drawings we see he designed various options for the furniture but the layout of the room is consistent with his floor plan. He opted for a grand four-poster bed with built in cabinets that dominated the room. It has gilded flame finials, gilded Greek key border on a platform base, and a headboard in a gilded Chinese key form that frames a cheetah print upholstered center. The headboard was set into an alcove with matching cheetah print wall covering and a large blue and gold family crest mounted above. The interior sides of the alcove housed small niches allowing for candles, objects and hiding places. Mont utilized his hide-a-way bar designs he did for the Mob and various Prohibition patrons to design a state bed with hidden compartments. The equally massive built in cabinets with gilded moldings and bronze hardware completes the state bed's structure.

Facing the state bed was a monumental mirrored console with an attached canopy and matches the grandeur of the bed. This, too, is on a plinth but it extends beyond the console, allowing two square fluted columns to rise up and support the canopy. A Greek key pattern borders the plinth and canopy, and Asian symbol square knobs adorn the drawers but in a larger scale.

In typical Mont fashion, exotic luxury spilled onto the patio. A lush scene with stone Buddha, bronze Roman busts, a gilded bamboo wall and a large stone fountain graced the exterior of the Orlowitz penthouse. The space was divided in two by a white fence with a Chinoiserie lattice pattern and vines meandering throughout. One side had a

THE ORLOWITZ COLLECTION
FROM THE KING COLE PENTHOUSE
MIAMI BEACH

Roman feel, with travertine floors, bronze busts, large potted palms and iron furniture. The other side was like a Zen garden, with a heavily lacquered brick floor in a spiral pattern, which was designed to emulate a giant redwood tree and was the Orlowitz's dance floor. The dance floor ended with a gravel floor dotted with amoeba shaped stepping-stones that led to the large stone fountain. The greenery was less structured, almost overgrown; and the smiling stone Buddha that peeked from bushes, the gilded bamboo walls and the mini pagodas created a calming yet cheerful outdoor setting.

Ellis Orlowitz loved Mont's style and eccentric personality and understood James Mont's vision; the two played cards and gambled together often. He allowed Mont to create a home fit for a king, which Mont did. Unfortunately, Mont's temperamental personality resulted in an unknown, "beyond his control" circumstance that forced him to quit at the eleventh hour. If he hadn't mysteriously ceased operations, Mrs. Orlowitz would not have hired a replacement designer and all of Mont's designs would have come to fruition. Luckily, the architectural drawings and original contract document Mont's design and allow us to see his vision firsthand.

The original 1963 contract lists all the furniture Mont specified and is coupled with a letter stating the job was 90% complete. Mont finished the entire interior architecture down to the last detail: niches, hidden compartments, fretwork and doorknobs were all installed, walls were painted, cornices were gilded, marble floors and shag carpet were laid, and the patio was completed.

Through time-consuming and delicate restoration, Todd Merrill Antiques has brought the Orlowitz furniture collection back to its intended look, using the same techniques Mont employed, thus giving this collection new life in its original design.

Essay by Erin Johnson for Todd Merrill & Associates, Inc.

EXHIBITION & SALE CATALOG

THE KING COLE PENTHOUSE

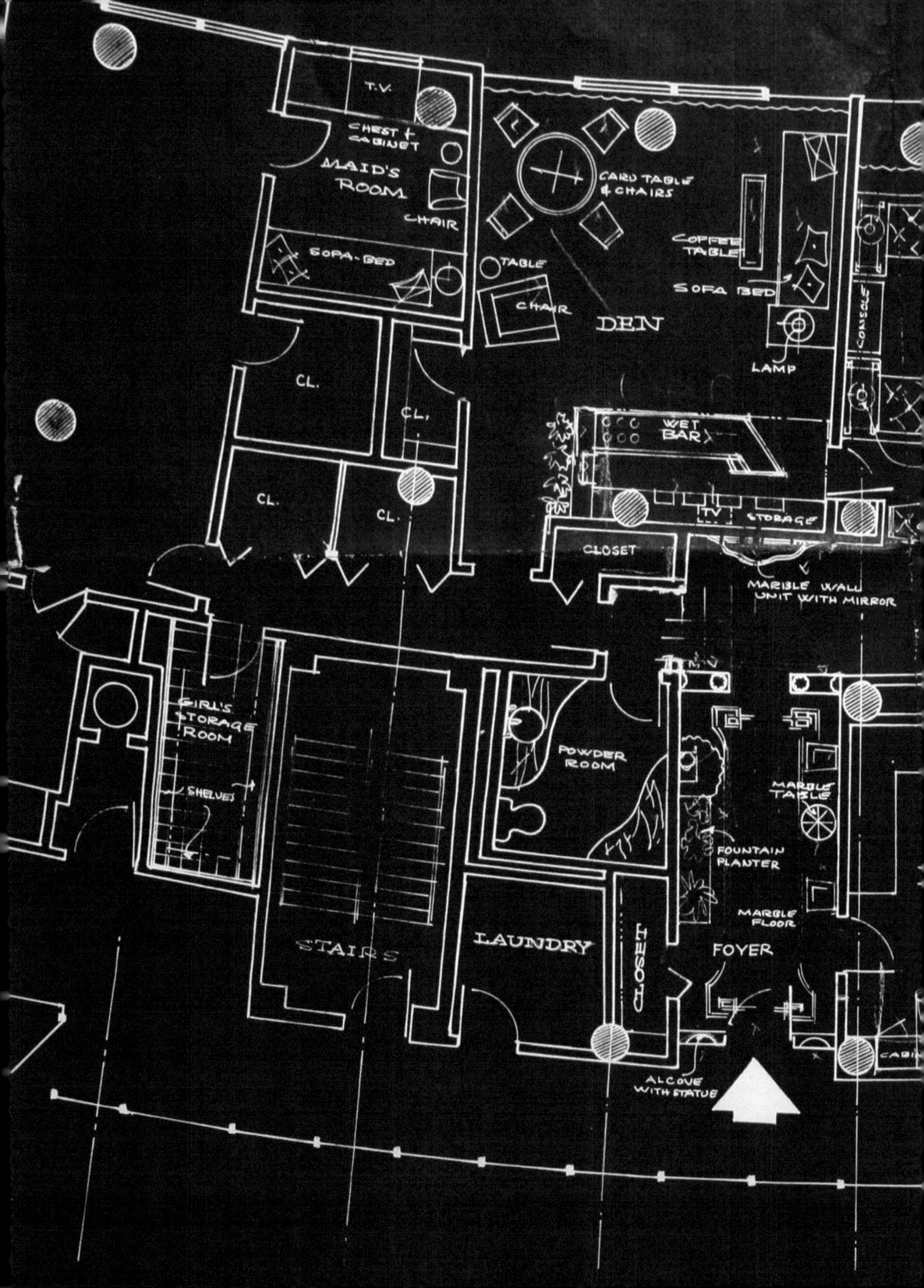

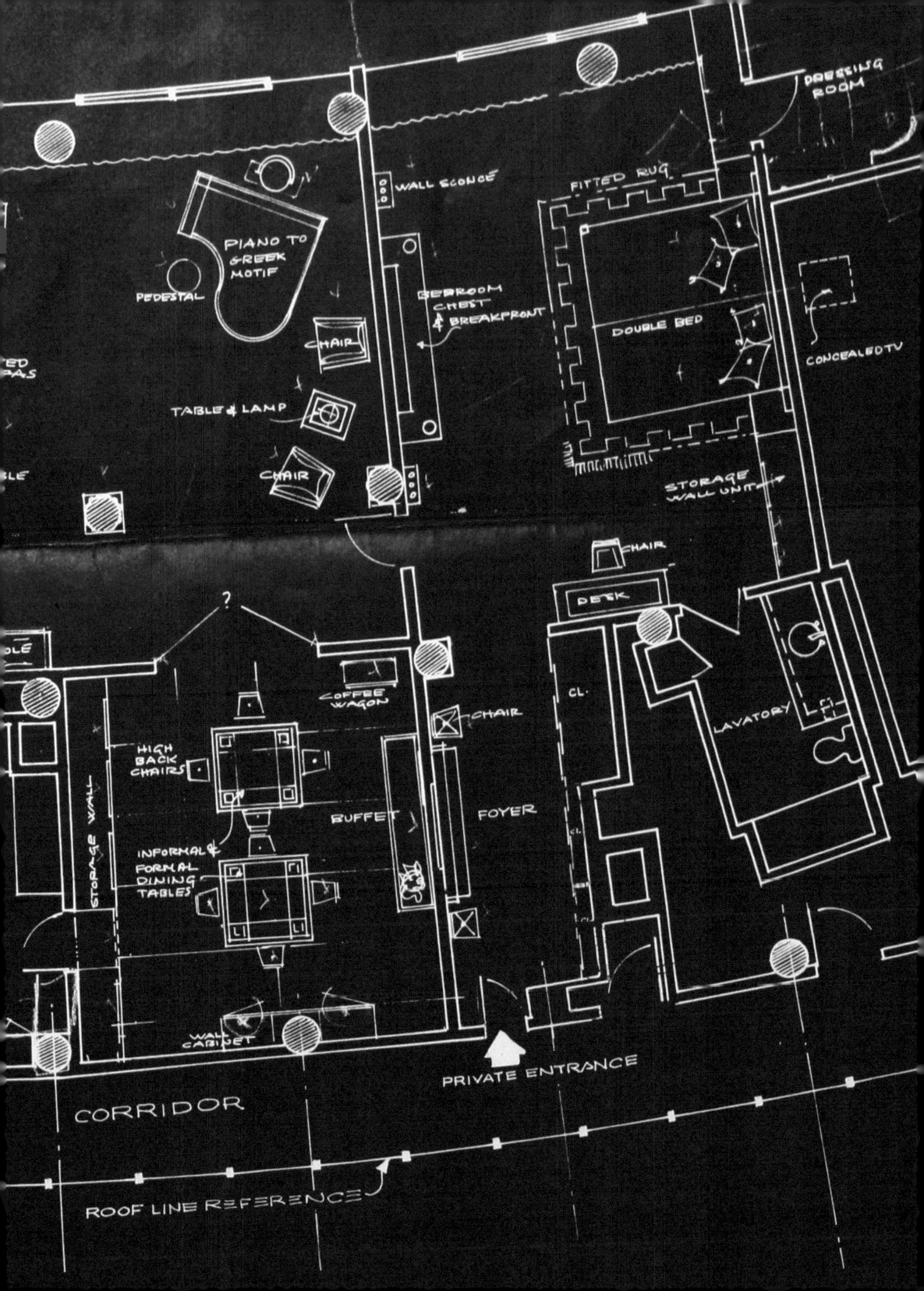

DINING ROOM

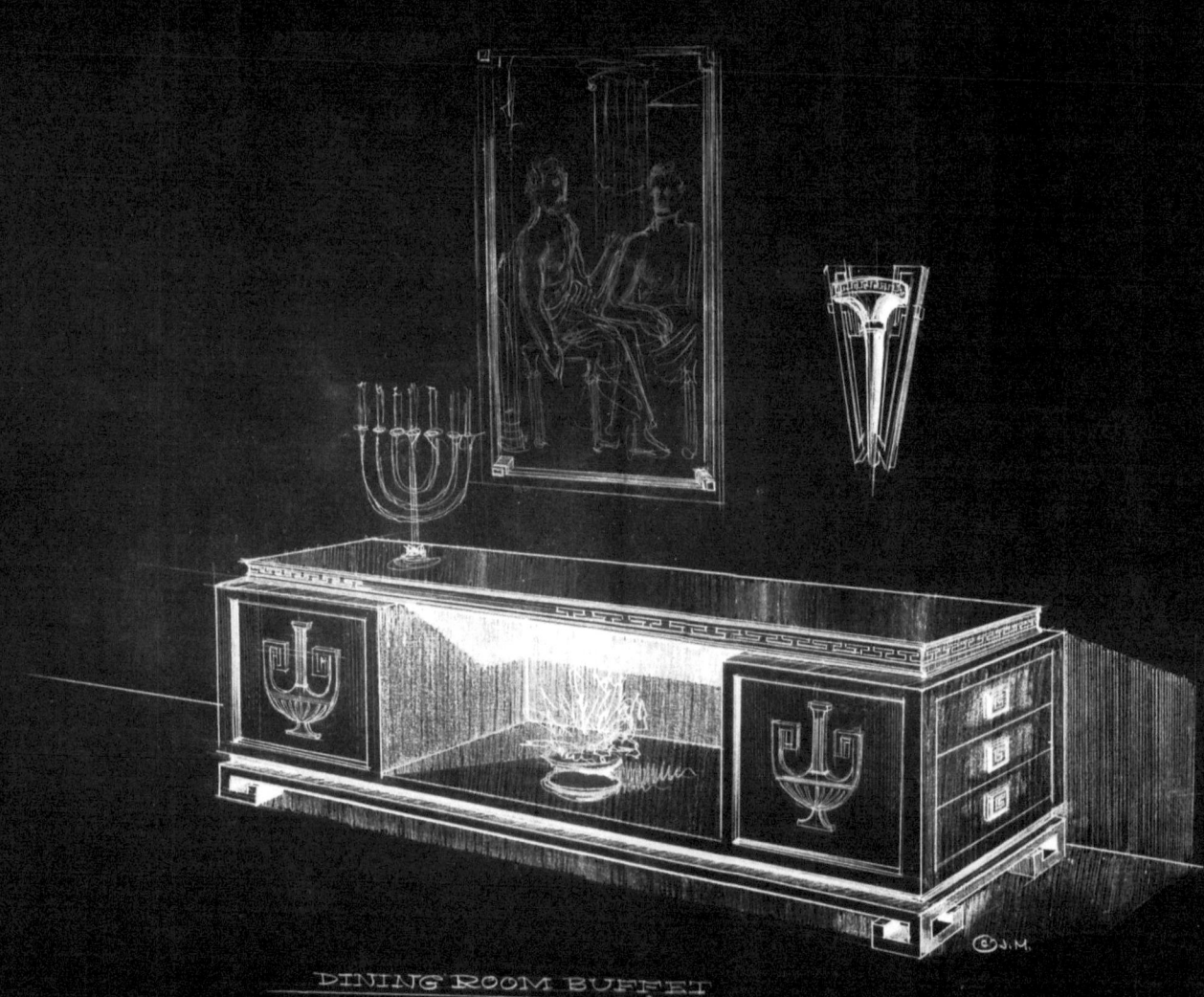

Dwg. 7
Perspective drawing of dining room buffet of Orlowitz King Cole Penthouse by James Mont, ca 1963.

Dwg. 6
Perspective drawing of a proposed dual dining table of Orlowitz King Cole Penthouse by James Mont, ca. 1963.

Dining Table

With an antiqued smoked-mirror top and Chinoiserie fretwork carved apron, on a single fluted column pedestal with a Greek key base. Finished in antiqued gold metal leaf. Accompanied by a copy of the original concept drawing of the Orlowitz dining room signed by James Mont. Listed on Mont's Contract Specifications provided by Mont to Mr. Orlowitz.

New York, 1963

41"H x 86"L x 44"D

Provenance:
Ellis Orlowitz, King Cole Penthouse, Miami Beach, USA
Mr. Steven Z. Levinson & Dr. Judi Berson-Levinson, King Cole Penthouse, Miami Beach, USA

Item Number: TMF823

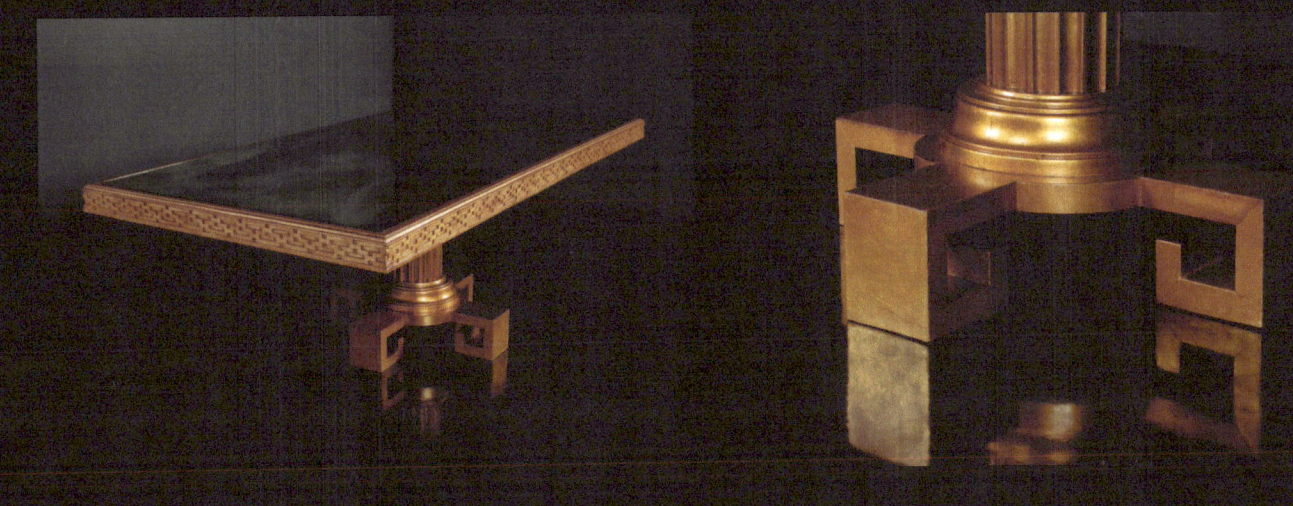

Set of 8 High-Back Dining Chairs

Each with elongated Greek key backs and Chinoiserie fretwork carved apron, each finished in satin black lacquer with gold leaf detail. Seats retain original horsehair filling upholstered with new grey silk velvet and silk satin piping.

Accompanied by a copy of the original concept drawing of the Orlowitz dining room signed by James Mont. Listed on Mont's Contract Specifications provided by Mont to Mr. Orlowitz.

New York, 1963

41"H x 19.5"L x 19"D

Provenance:
Ellis Orlowitz, King Cole Penthouse, Miami Beach, USA
Mr. Steven Z. Levinson & Dr. Judi Berson-Levinson, King Cole Penthouse, Miami Beach, USA

Item Number: TMF824

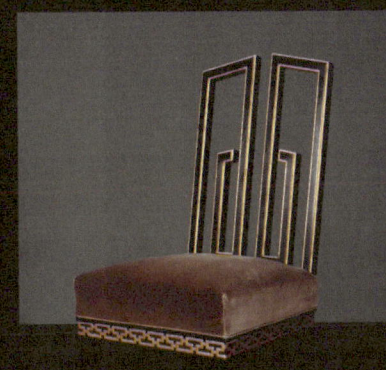

Dining Console

Top inset with smoked-mirror panel into a gold metal leaf frame with Chinoiserie fretwork carved edge, mounted on top of an antiqued silver leaf cabinet inset with two smoked-mirror panels, each panel with carved Classical urn gold metal leaf appliqué, three mirrored drawers on each end of the sideboard that rests on a Greek key base.

Accompanied by a copy of the original concept drawing signed by James Mont. Listed on Mont's Contract Specifications provided by Mont to Mr. Orlowitz.

New York, 1963

30.5"H x 94.5"L x 22"D

Provenance:
Ellis Orlowitz, King Cole Penthouse, Miami Beach, USA
Mr. Steven Z. Levinson & Dr. Judi Berson-Levinson, King Cole Penthouse, Miami Beach, USA

Item Number: TMF825

LIVING ROOM

Long Sofa

Rare antiqued silver leaf three-sectioned sofa, one-person sections flank a four-person section with unusual arms carved with Classical and Asian decorative motifs, upholstered in tufted grey silk velvet. Typical of Mont's work, vintage or antique parts appears to have been incorporated in the sofa's construction. Listed on Mont's Contract Specifications provided by Mont to Mr. Orlowitz.

New York, 1963

31"H x 120"L x 32"D

Provenance:
Ellis Orlowitz, King Cole Penthouse, Miami Beach, USA
Mr. Steven Z. Levinson & Dr. Judi Berson-Levinson, King Cole Penthouse, Miami Beach, USA

Item Number: TMF826

Pair of Club Chairs

Each with pierced fretwork arms and back, finished in black lacquer and detailed with gold leaf, upholstered in grey silk velvet. These chairs are listed in the original scope of work provided by Mont to Mr. Orlowitz.

New York, 1963

27.5"H x 26.5"L x 29"D

Provenance:
Ellis Orlowitz, King Cole Penthouse, Miami Beach, USA
Mr. Steven Z. Levinson & Dr. Judi Berson-Levinson, King Cole Penthouse, Miami Beach, USA

Item Number: TMF827

Corinthian Low Table

Round smoked-mirror top with gold metal leaf Chinoiserie fretwork carved apron mounted on an antique iron Corinthian capital base finished in gold metal leaf. The base of this table is reputed to be a "found" item from a bank building in New York City. Mont often incorporated antique items as decorative elements in his furniture. This table is shown placed in the furnished floor plan of the apartment as laid out by James Mont.

New York, 1963.

16.5"H x 48.5"DIA

Provenance:
Ellis Orlowitz, King Cole Penthouse, Miami Beach, USA
Mr. Steven Z. Levinson & Dr. Judi Berson-Levinson, King Cole Penthouse, Miami Beach, USA

Item Number: TMF828

Low Table

Square top decorated with Chinoiserie fretwork carved apron on a fluted column base, finished in antiqued gold metal leaf as shown in concept drawing. Listed on Mont's Contract Specifications provided by Mont to Mr. Orlowitz.

New York, 1963

19.5"H x 21.5"L x 21.5"D

Provenance:
Ellis Orlowitz, King Cole Penthouse, Miami Beach, USA
Mr. Steven Z. Levinson & Dr. Judi Berson-Levinson, King Cole Penthouse, Miami Beach, USA

Item Number: TMF829

Lotus Low Table

Round top with Chinoiserie fretwork carved apron on a beautifully carved column pedestal and Lotus motif base, finished in silver leaf with gold leaf accents. Accompanied by a copy of the original concept drawing of the Orlowitz living room.

New York, 1963

15.5"H x 30"DIA

Provenance:
Ellis Orlowitz, King Cole Penthouse, Miami Beach, USA
Mr. Steven Z. Levinson & Dr. Judi Berson-Levinson, King Cole Penthouse, Miami Beach, USA

Item Number: TMF838

Pair of Cabinets

In the style of James Mont, both with smoked-mirror tops, two-doors with gilt bronze lion head hardware, classical column mounts, finished in gold and silver metal leaf and faded, smoked lacquer.

These cabinets appears on Mont's original floor plan and Contract Specifications for the Orlowitz penthouse, and may have been designed by Mont; but were probably produced after the original installation.

20.5"H x 41.25"L x 16"D

Provenance:
Ellis Orlowitz, King Cole Penthouse, Miami Beach, USA
Sheri Orlowitz, Miami, FL, USA

Item Number: TMF975

Turned Lamps

Turned column forms in smoked-lacquer, gold on silver metal leaf camouflage pattern finish with matching silver leaf shades. Listed on Mont's Contract Specifications provided by Mont for Mr. Orlowitz.

42.5"H x 15.5"DIA (shade)

Provenance:
Ellis Orlowitz, King Cole Penthouse, Miami Beach, USA
Sheri Orlowitz, Miami, FL, USA

Item Number: TML328

Long Console

In the style of James Mont, a smoked-mirror top rests on eight classical column supports, finished in silver and gold metal-leaf camouflage pattern and faded, smoked lacquer.

This console appears on Mont's original floor plan and Contract Specifications for the Orlowitz penthouse, and may have been designed by Mont; but was probably produced after the original installation.

25.5"H x 82"L x 20"D

Provenance:
Ellis Orlowitz, King Cole Penthouse, Miami Beach, USA
Sheri Orlowitz, Miami, FL, USA

Item Number: TMF974

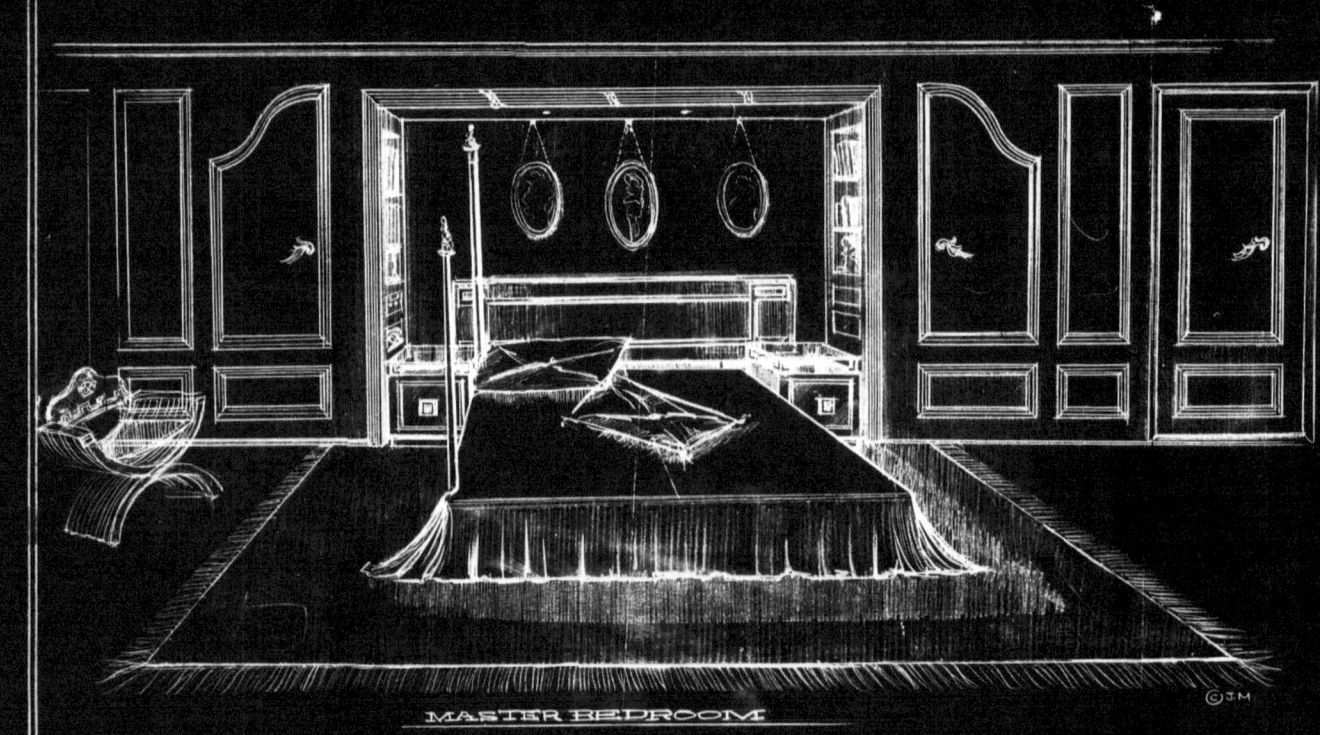

Dwg. 10
Perspective drawing of bed in the Master
Bedroom of Orlowitz King Cole Penthouse
by James Mont, ca 1963.

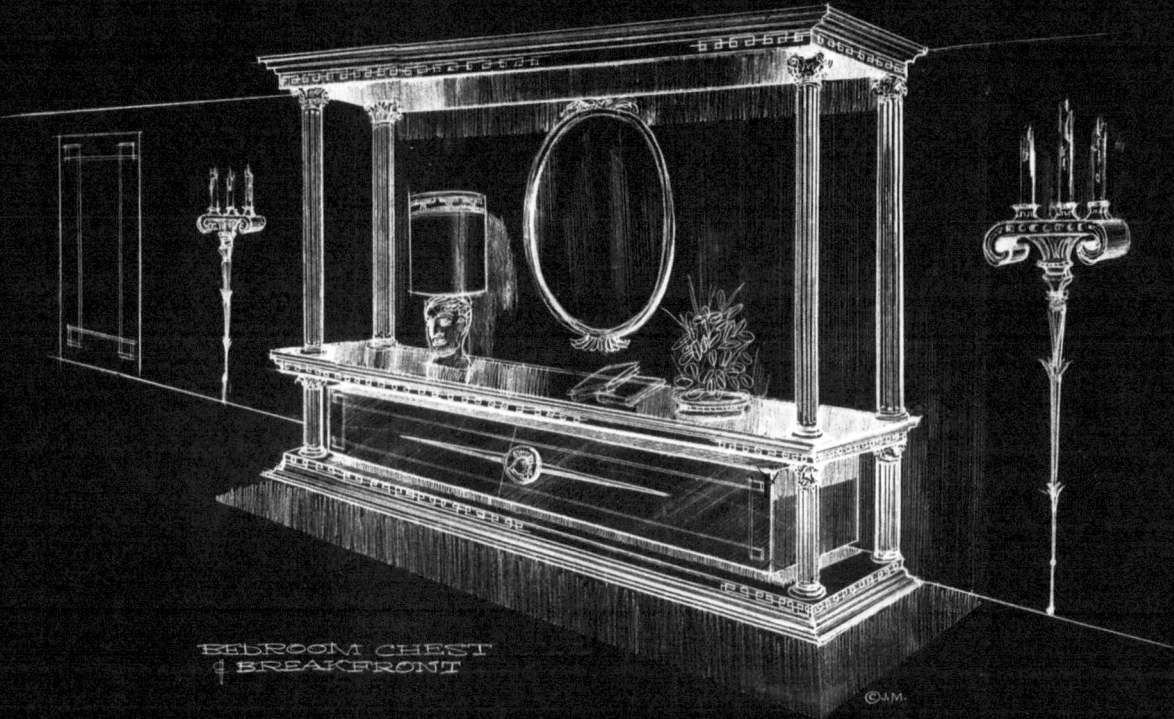

Dwg. 11
Perspective drawing of bedroom chest
of Orlowitz King Cole Penthouse
by James Mont, ca.1963.

Monumental Chest of Drawers

Oversized chest in the manner of a Greco-Roman sarcophagus, with architectural canopy supported by square fluted columns, all mounted on a platform base decorated with carved Greek-key in gold leaf. The chest features five deep drawers with carved fretwork gilded pulls and canopy features a recessed light, finished in silver leaf. The center drawer has two burned in marks James Mont Designs. Accompanied by an original concept drawing of this chest for Orlowitz signed by James Mont. Listed on Mont's Contract Specifications.

New York, 1963

99"H x 129"L x 23"D

Provenance:
Ellis Orlowitz, King Cole Penthouse, Miami Beach, USA
Mr. Steven Z. Levinson & Dr. Judi Berson-Levinson, King Cole Penthouse, Miami Beach, USA

Item Number: TMF831

Important King-Size Four Poster Bed

Includes a pierced carved grey silk velvet upholstered headboard both with silver leaf finish, each post decorated with gilded and carved flame finials. The entire bed rests on a platform base decorated with carved classical Greek key in gold leaf. Accompanied by a copy of the original concept drawing of the Orlowitz Master bedroom including this bed signed by James Mont. Listed on Mont's Contract Specifications.

New York, 1963

79"H x 83"L x 87"D

Provenance:
Ellis Orlowitz, King Cole Penthouse, Miami Beach, USA
Mr. Steven Z. Levinson & Dr. Judi Berson-Levinson, King Cole Penthouse, Miami Beach, USA

Console

Features two cabinets with doors and one center false cabinet, doors mounted with pierced, carved and gilded square pulls, all on a platform base, finished in gold on silver leaf camouflage pattern. Shown on the original furnished floor plan by James Mont and listed on Mont's Contract Specifications.

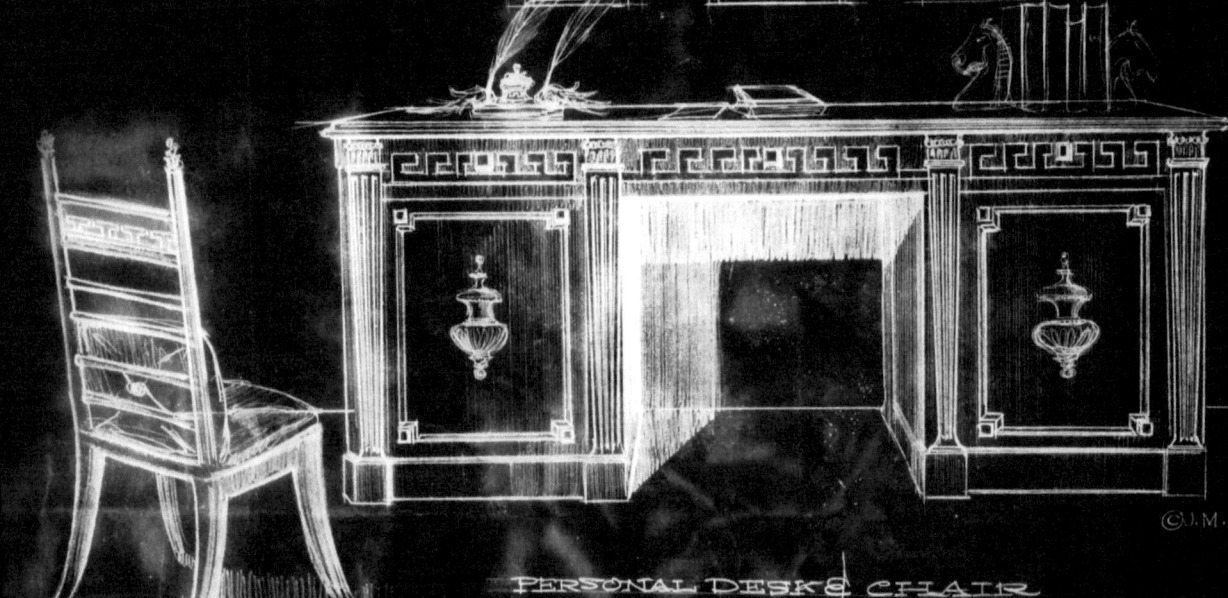

PERSONAL DESK & CHAIR

Writing Desk And Chair

Classically inspired with gold on silver leaf camouflage patterned top with gilded Greek key fretwork carved apron, double pedestal base features two cabinets in silver leaf with carved and gilded Venetian lion's head mounts. The desk accompanied by the original Klismos chair finished in gold on silver leaf camouflage pattern, upholstered in gold silk velvet.

Accompanied by a copy of the original concept drawing of this desk for Orlowitz signed by James Mont. Listed on Mont's Contract Specifications.

New York, 1963

Desk: 30.5"H x 61"L x 23"D
Chair: 36"H x 22"L x 23"D

Provenance:
Ellis Orlowitz, King Cole Penthouse, Miami Beach, USA
Mr. Steven Z. Levinson & Dr. Judi Berson-Levinson, King Cole Penthouse, Miami Beach, USA

Item Number: TMF832

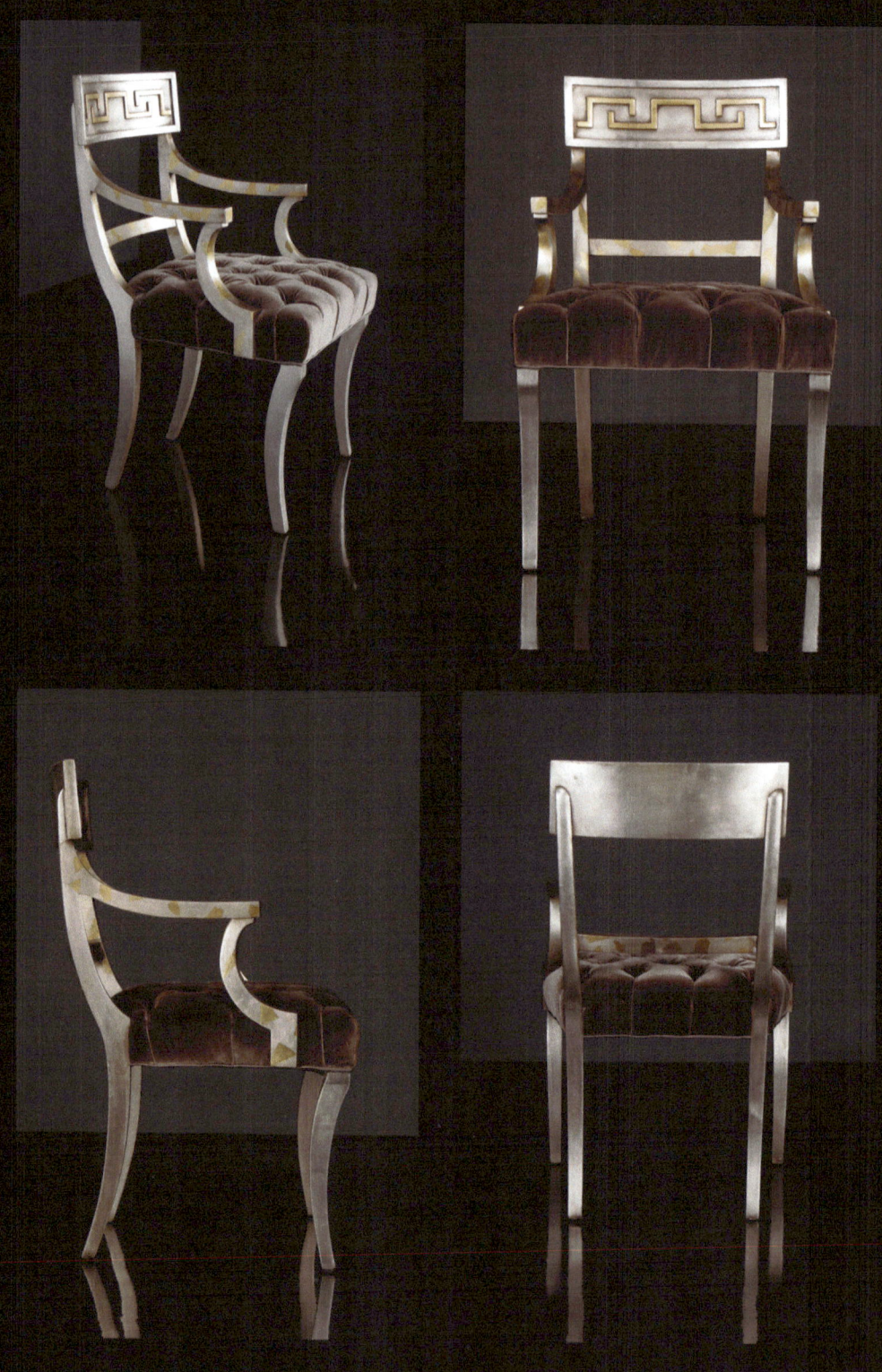

Dwg. 13
Perspective drawing of Chinoiserie
Bar of Orlowitz King Cole Penthouse
by James Mont, ca.1963.

Gaming Table

Table features a flip top that opens and slides to double its size, top rests on Asian inspired legs in an X-form, finished in orange faded cinnabar lacquer. Listed on Mont's Contract Specifications.

New York, 1963

27"H x 35"L (closed) x 70"L (open) x 35"D

Provenance:
Ellis Orlowitz, King Cole Penthouse, Miami Beach, USA
Mr. Steven Z. Levinson & Dr. Judi Berson-Levinson, King Cole Penthouse, Miami Beach, USA

Item Number: TMF835

Set of Eight Gaming or Dining Chairs

Magnificently designed, Chinese inspired chairs with circular bent wood backs and legs, each finished in antiqued gold metal leaf over a terracotta base. One chair is a custom reproduction. Listed on Mont's Contract Specifications.

New York, 1963

27.5"H x 23"L x 23.5"D

Provenance:
Ellis Orlowitz, King Cole Penthouse, Miami Beach, USA
Mr. Steven Z. Levinson & Dr. Judi Berson-Levinson, King Cole Penthouse, Miami Beach, USA

Item Number: TMF836

Console

Comprising three parts, two low cabinets flank a taller center cabinet, beautifully constructed and finished in a high polished "piano" black lacquer with a large Chinoiserie silvered bronze medallion pull.

New York, 1963

35"H x 82"L x 27"D

Provenance:
Ellis Orlowitz, King Cole Penthouse, Miami Beach, USA
Mr. Steven Z. Levinson & Dr. Judi Berson-Levinson, King Cole Penthouse, Miami Beach, USA

Item Number: TMF837

Opium Den Sofa And Low Table

Upholstered one-arm sofa rests on a long platform in silver leaf over orange and black primer on oak with antiqued lacquer finish. The effect is gilded bronze.

Low table accompanies the "opium den" sofa in matching silver leaf over orange and black primer on oak with antiqued lacquer finish. Listed on Mont's Contract Specifications.

Identical in form to the one listed in Eric Philippe's October 2004 Exhibition page 51.

New York, designed ca.1948, this piece executed in 1963 with custom finish for Ellis Orlowitz

Sofa: 28"H x 90.5"L x 36.5"D - 112"L x 40"D base
Low Table: 12.5"H x 53"L x 26"D

Provenance:
Ellis Orlowitz, King Cole Penthouse, Miami Beach, USA
Sheri Orlowitz, Miami, FL, USA

Item Number: TMF957

Small Lamp

Sculpted bass wood patinated silver leaf over black base with faded silver leaf shade.

Height   20"
Shade Diameter   16"

Provenance:
Ellis Orlowitz, King Cole Penthouse, Miami Beach, USA
Sheri Orlowitz, Miami, FL, USA

Item Number: TML329

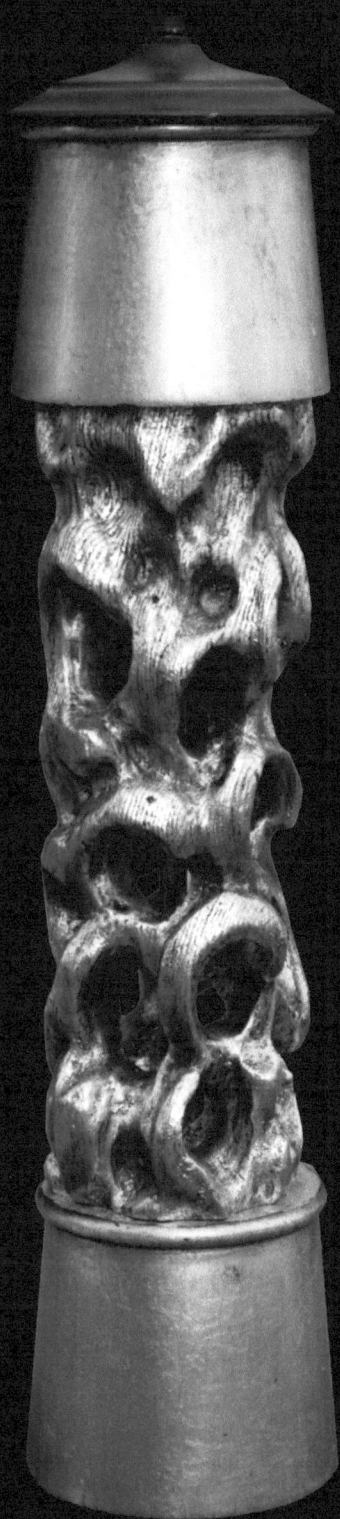

78

OTHER JAMES MONT ITEMS

Console / Vanity

A slender console/vanity with hidden pop-up mirror, gilt bamboo latticework applied to the two front drawers. Burned in marked inside both drawers James Mont Designs.

Circa 1940

28"H (35.25"H open) x 60"L x 16"D

Item Number: TMF976

Gold And Silver Lamps

Stacked graduated balls, finished in gold and silver leaf with matching gold and silver leaf shades.

Circa 1940

41"H x 19"DIA (shade)

Item Number: TMF328

85

Tub Chairs

Finished in silver leaf and black with black patent leather upholstery.

29"H x 27"L x 24"D

Provenance:
The Levine Collection

Item Number: TMF814

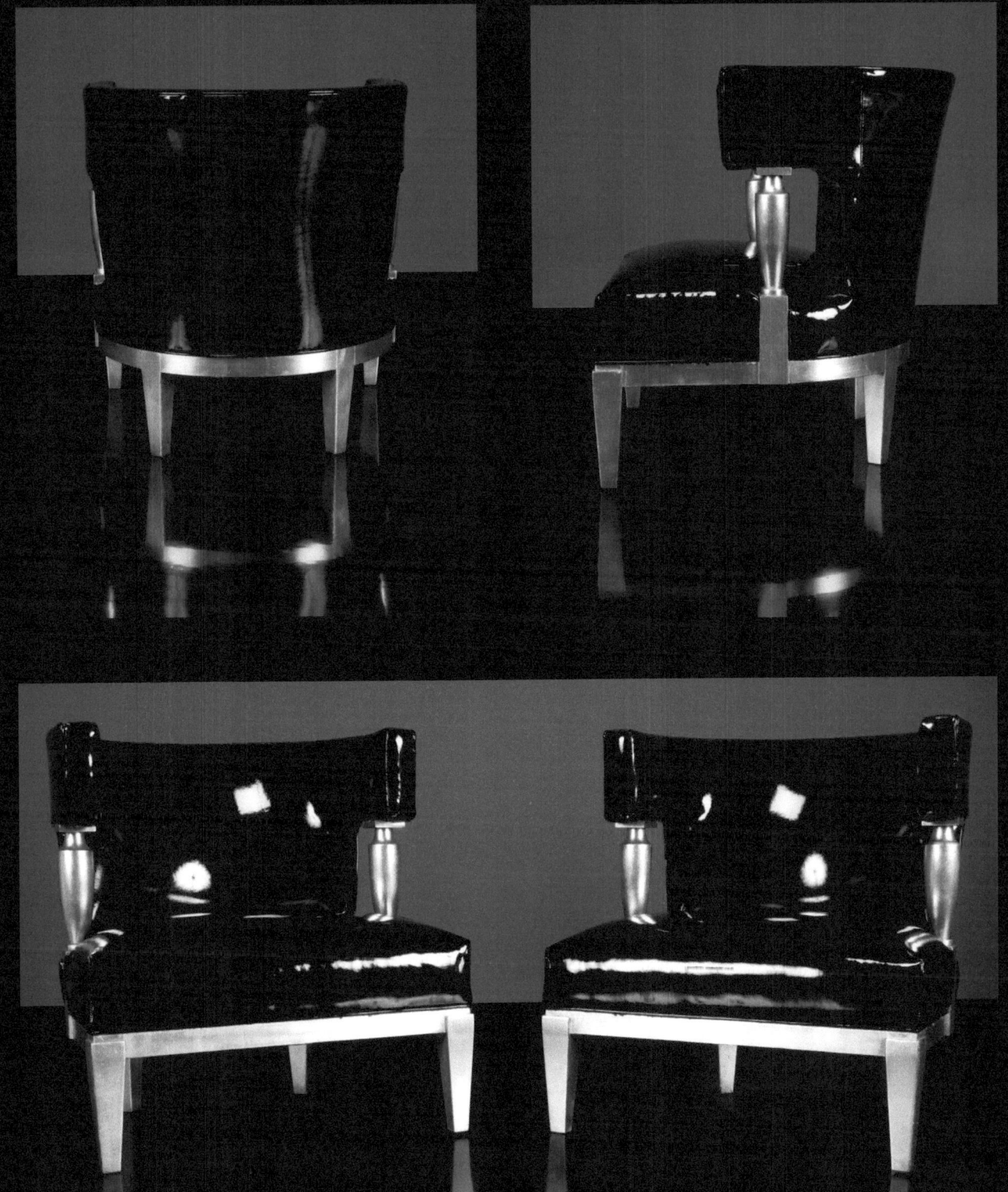

Console Server

An important cinnabar lacquered and gilded Chinoiserie console server designed and built in the late 1950's. This piece reflects an interesting convergence of Art Deco, Moderne and Asian design, which typifies James Mont's work. The centerpiece of the cabinet is an antique Chinese carved and gilded screen or grill backed by smoked mirror. This cabinet is one of several pieces of furniture that was created using related Chinese architectural elements. This console is nearly identical to a black lacquer version sold at Rago Galleries. The console is comprised of four pieces, the base is one unit with a large drawer flanked by two cabinets, the top center is a shallow decorative Chinoiserie grill flanked by two cabinets with gilded faux lanterns mounted on each. The cabinet was originally purchased from Mont's showroom in Manhattan for a Sutton Place, Manhattan apartment.

79"H x 78"L x 20"D

Item Number: TMF375

Pair of Dressers

Each has a wavy front comprising four drawers and finished in silver leaf over black base with carved black lacquer and silver leaf pulls.

Burned in mark on inside top drawer James Mont Designs.

Circa 1950's

34"H x 46"L x 18"D

Item Number: TMF960

Pagoda End Tables

Each in a Pagoda three-tiered form with black high polish lacquer finish.
Identical to the ones listed in Eric Philippe's October 2004 Exhibition page 21.

Burned in mark on underside of table James Mont Designs.

Circa 1950's

Longest tables: 7"H (8.25" top of flare) x 36"L x 13"D
Medium tables: 7"H (8.25" top of flare) x 26.75"L x 13"D
Shortest tables: 7"H (8.25" top of flare) x 18.25"L x 13"D

Item Number TMF962

Seated Asian Figural Lamp

An Asian figure in gilded ceramic, wood, paper and carved plaster with gold leaf finish. Heavy paper gold leaf shade with decorative ring of applied and carved plaster.

Circa 1940's

46"H x 17"DIA (shade)

Item Number: TML158

Lamp

Carved and silver gilt faux bamboo lamp with black and white silk shade.

Circa 1950's

34"H x 18"DIA

Item Number: TML180

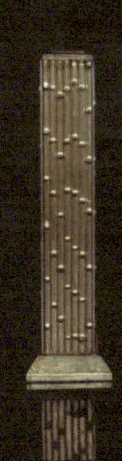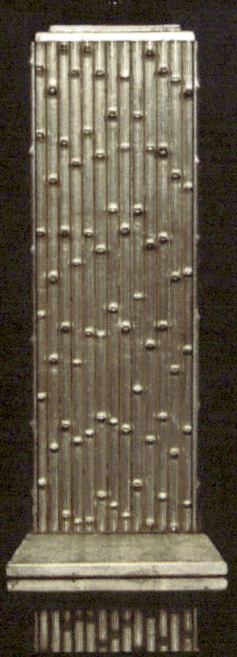

Exceptional Pair of Lamps

In bleached carved mahogany with original gilt shades.

Circa 1950's

42"H x 18.5"DIA (Shade)

Item Number: TML287

Asian Figural Lamp

An Asian figure carved in driftwood with multi-layered hand rubbed gilded finish in tones of pale blue, gray and variegated gold. Original hand painted and gilded parchment shade.

Circa 1950's

52"H x 20"DIA (Shade)

Item Number: TML250

Standing Bar

Early solid whitewashed and bleached oak hand-carved and dovetailed bar with tipple folding front door, with bronze hardware. Features mirrored interior with orange lacquer and hand-carved, hand-dovetailed drawers. Burned in marked into underside of bronze pull James Mont Designs.

Green Desk

An elegantly proportioned compact executive desk with original leather top, bronze hardware, mounts finished in green stain over oak. Comprises nine drawers, four on each side with a center drawer, bronze banding around the on all side, designed to float in a room. Burned in mark in center drawer and stamped on each of the nine pulls James Mont Designs.

30"H x 48"L x 24"D

Item Number: TMF411

CONCEPT DRAWINGS

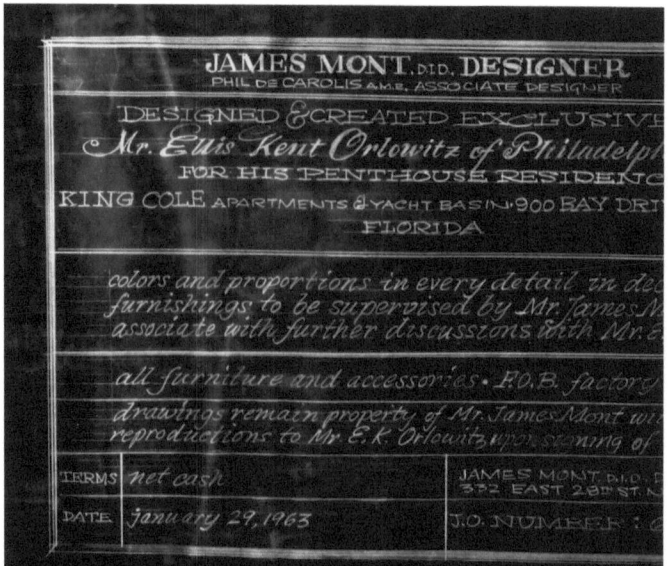

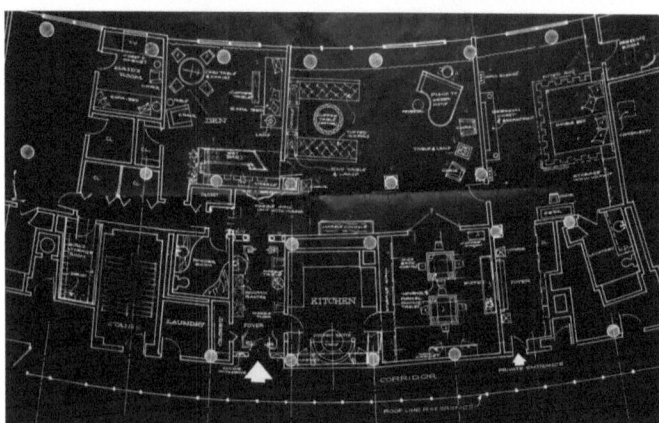

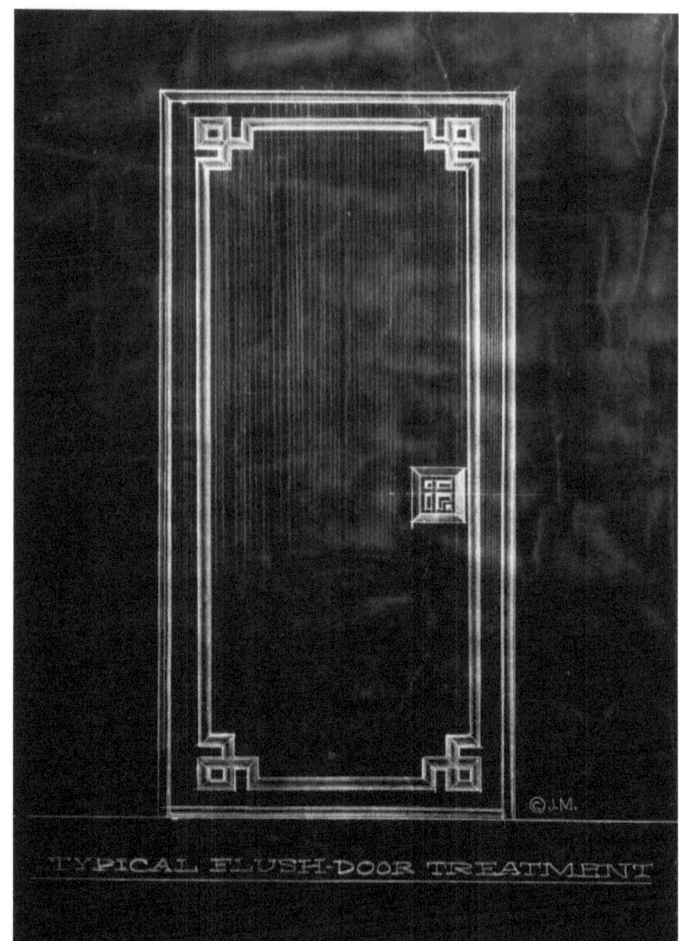

Dwg. 1
Titleblock and "contract for work" for Orlowitz King Cole Penthouse by James Mont, ca. 1963.

Dwg. 2
Original floor plan of Orlowitz King Cole Penthouse by James Mont, ca. 1963.

Dwg. 3
Drawing of typical door treatment of Orlowitz King Cole Penthouse by James Mont, ca.1963.

Dwg. 4
Elevation drawing of front entrance of Orlowitz King Cole Penthouse by James Mont, ca 1963.

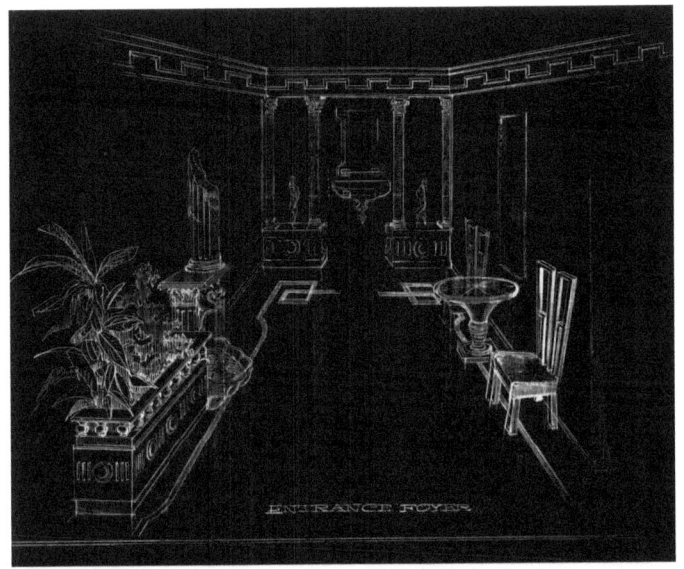

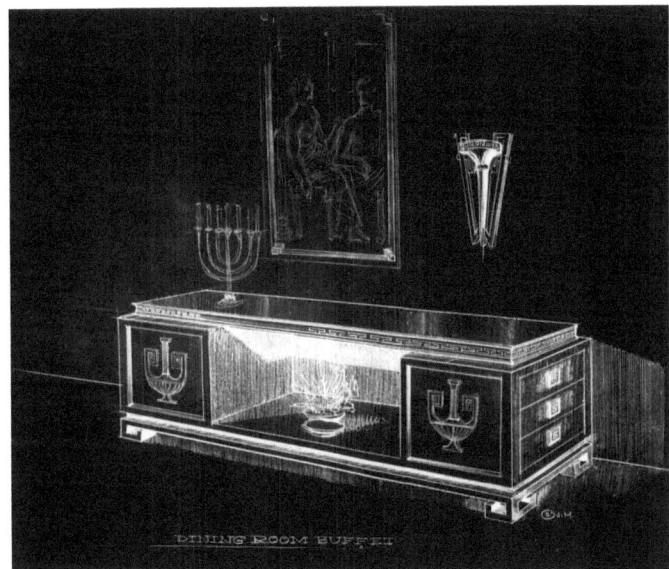

Dwg. 5
Perspective drawing of foyer of Orlowitz King Cole Penthouse by James Mont, ca 1963.

Dwg. 6
Perspective drawing proposed dual dining table of Orlowitz King Cole Penthouse by James Mont, ca. 1963.

Dwg. 7
Perspective drawing of living room buffet of Orlowitz King Cole Penthouse by James Mont, ca 1963.

Dwg. 8
Perspective drawing of dining room buffet of Orlowitz King Cole Penthouse by James Mont, ca 1963.

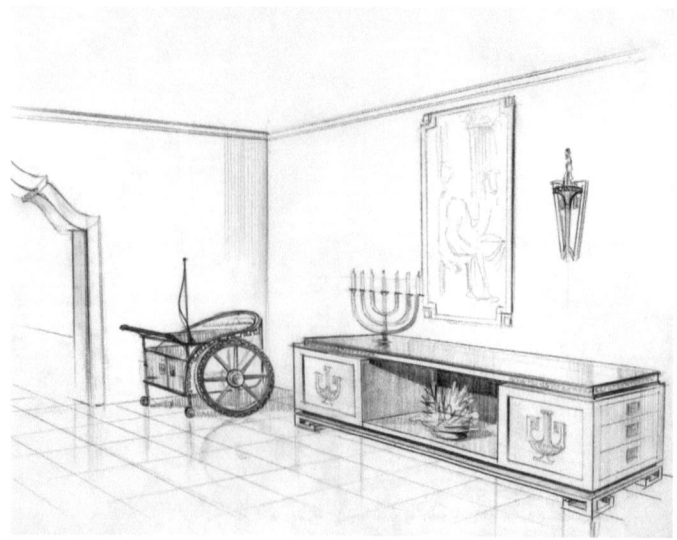

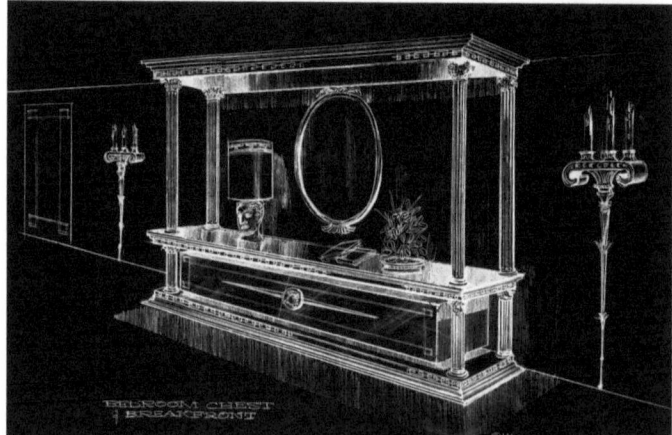

Dwg. 9
Perspective drawing of chariot bar cart and dining room buffet of Orlowitz King Cole Penthouse by James Mont, ca 1963.

Dwg. 10
Perspective drawing of Chinoiserie Bar of Orlowitz King Cole Penthouse by James Mont, ca 1963.

Dwg. 11
Perspective drawing of master bedroom writing desk and chair of Orlowitz King Cole Penthouse by James Mont, ca.1963.

Dwg. 12
Perspective drawing of bedroom chest of Orlowitz King Cole Penthouse by James Mont, ca.1963.

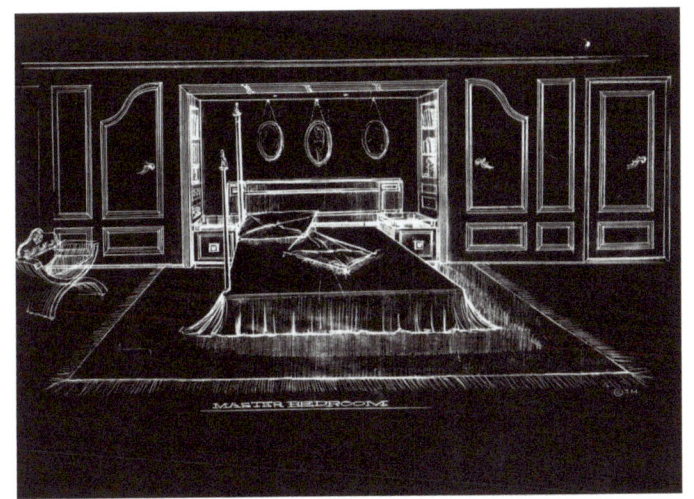
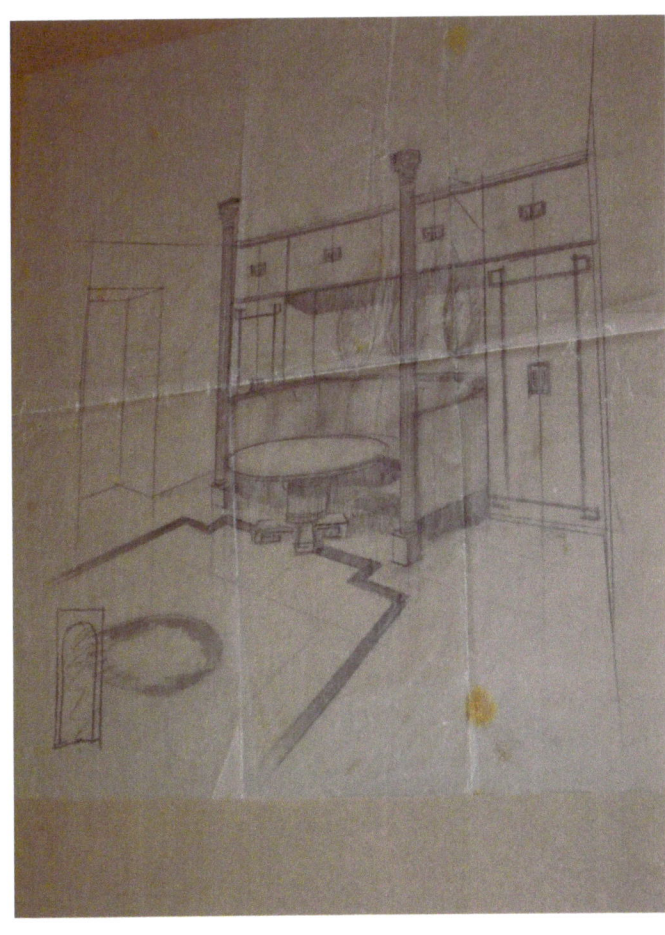

Dwg. 13
Perspective drawing of bed in the Master Bedroom of Orlowitz King Cole Penthouse by James Mont, ca.1963.

Dwg. 14
Perspective drawing of kitchen eating area of Orlowitz King Cole Penthouse by James Mont, ca.1963.

BIBLIOGRAPHY

Art Digest. "Turkish Designer Produces Modern Décor." Volume 9, October 15, 1934: pg 14.

Cartier, Inc. letter to James Mont, July 1, 1966.

Contract between James Mont and Ellis K. Orlowitz, signed by Orlowitz, initialed by Mont, dated February 4, 1963.

Chicago Daily Tribune. "Note to Husband May be Clew [sic] to Beauty's Suicide." April 26, 1937: p18.

———. "He Does Everything For Stranded Pair Except Marry Them." June 3, 1948: p 1.

Friedlend, Jerry, interviewed by Todd Merrill and Erin Johnson, July 5, 2007, transcript, Todd Merrill & Associates, New York, NY.

Greenfield, June, interviewed by Erin Johnson, September 13, 2007.

Karma, Inez. "Cocktail Party Namesmanship." New York Times. March 18, 1956: p 244.

Los Angeles Times. "Actress Suicide and Joke Party Linked by Odd Quirk of Fate." April 26, 1937: p 1.

———. "Actress' Death Puzzle Cleared." May 2, 1937: p 3.

Mont, James. letter to the editor. New York Times. March 7, 1936: p14.

Mont, James. 1937. Design for Service Bar. US Patent 106,317, filed August 25, 1937, and issued October 5, 1937.

Mont, James. 1947. Design for a Sofa. US Patent 152,720, filed February 5, 1947, and issued February 15, 1949. (references cited on patent: Montgomery Ward & Co.,

Catalog No. 131, 1939-1940, sofa on right side of lower cut on page #477 and davenport in left center of page #481)

Mont, James. 1953. Portable Bar. US Patent 171,856, filed November 3, 1953, and issued March 30, 1954.

Mont, James. The Young Physician's Road Map. New York, NY: Modern Mode   Furniture Co., Inc., no date.

New York Times. "Apartment Leases." January 26, 1932: p 42.

———. "Business Records, Judgments." May 25, 1933: p 37.

———. "Business Records." October 29, 1934: p 24.

———. "Hostess Ends Life as 100 Guests Wait." April 25, 1937: p1.

———. "Lans Galleries get Lehne Building." November 19, 1938: p 30.

———. "Court Firm on High Bail." November 26, 1939: p 43.

———. "Space-Saving Devices to Expand a Tiny Apartment." December 24, 1945: p 12.

Art Digest. "Turkish Designer Produces Modern Décor." Volume 9, October 15, 1934: pg 14.

Cartier, Inc. letter to James Mont, July 1, 1966.

Contract between James Mont and Ellis K. Orlowitz, signed by Orlowitz, initialed by Mont, dated February 4, 1963.

Chicago Daily Tribune. "Note to Husband May be Clew [sic] to Beauty's Suicide." April 26, 1937: p18.

———. "He Does Everything For Stranded Pair Except Marry Them." June 3, 1948: p 1.

Friedlend, Jerry, interviewed by Todd Merrill and Erin Johnson, July 5, 2007, transcript, Todd Merrill & Associates, New York, NY.

Greenfield, June, interviewed by Erin Johnson, September 13, 2007.

Karma, Inez. "Cocktail Party Namesmanship." New York Times. March 18, 1956: p 244.

Los Angeles Times. "Actress Suicide and Joke Party Linked by Odd Quirk of Fate." April 26, 1937: p 1.

———. "Actress' Death Puzzle Cleared." May 2, 1937: p 3.

Mont, James. letter to the editor. New York Times. March 7, 1936: p14

Mont, James. 1937. Design for Service Bar. US Patent 106,317, filed August 25, 1937, and issued October 5, 1937.

Mont, James. 1947. Design for a Sofa. US Patent 152,720, filed February 5, 1947, and issued February 15, 1949. (references cited on patent: Montgomery Ward & Co., Catalog No. 131, 1939-1940, sofa on right side of lower cut on page #477 and davenport in left center of page #481)

Mont, James. 1953. Portable Bar. US Patent 171,856, filed November 3, 1953, and issued March 30, 1954.

Mont, James. The Young Physician's Road Map. New York, NY: Modern Mode   Furniture Co., Inc., no date.

New York Times. "Apartment Leases." January 26, 1932: p 42.

———. "Business Records, Judgments." May 25, 1933: p 37.

———. "Business Records." October 29, 1934: p 24.

———. "Hostess Ends Life as 100 Guests Wait." April 25, 1937: p1.

———. "Lans Galleries get Lehne Building." November 19, 1938: p 30.

———. "Court Firm on High Bail." November 26, 1939: p 43.

———. "Space-Saving Devices to Expand a Tiny Apartment." December 24, 1945: p 12.

———. "Display Advertisement." January 25, 1946: p 14.

———. "Business Records, Bankruptcy Proceedings." September 26, 1946: p 51.

———. "Oriental Motif Seen in Modern Furniture." November 20, 1946: p 38.

———. "Chair to be Auctioned." January 19, 1947: p 53.

———. "Roosevelt Birth Widely Observed." January 31, 1947: p 3.

———. "Advertisement." April 17, 1949: p 42.

———. "Manhattan Mortgages." January 5, 1950: p 51.

———. "Classifieds." March 28, 1951: p 39.

———. "Manhattan Transfers." March 27, 1952: p 51.

———. "Classifieds." April 20, 1952: p W18.

———. "Classifieds." June 1, 1952: p W14.

———. "Manhattan Mortgages." September 4, 1952: p 42.

———. "Manhattan Transfers." April 4, 1953: p 19.

———. "Manhattan Transfers." December 8, 1953: p 2.

———. "Manhattan Transfers." November 15, 1956: p 60.

———. "Musical is Added to Lerman's List." December 13, 1956: p 51.

Orlowitz, Sheri interviewed by Todd Merrill, August 23, 2007, transcript, Todd Merrill & Associates, New York, NY.

Owens, Mitchell. "Call It Auntie Mame Chinoiserie." New York Times. April 4, 1996:

Owens, Mitchell. "Godfather of Exotic Modernism." New York Times. October 6, 1996.

Owens, Mitchell. "Furniture a Gun Moll Would Have Found Just Swell." New York Times, June 15, 1997.

Roche, Mary. "Living-Dining Room Makes Available A Table With Plenty of Elbow Space." New York Times. June 12, 1945: p 16.

———. "Home, Accents and Contrasts." New York Times. July 1, 1945: p 61.

Schneider, Sondra. "Mid-Century Madness." Ocean Drive. November 2006: pp 332-338.

United Press. "London Docks Baby Assured Childhood Fit for Princess." Washington Post. November 20, 1948: p 1.

Villinsky, Beth. "James Mont: The Bad Boy of Mid-Century Modern." Christie's. June 10, 1997.

Washington Post. "Bride Ends Life as 100 Guests Wait." April 25, 1937: p 1.

www.ingramcontent.com/pod-product-compliance
Lightning Source LLC
Chambersburg PA
CBHW040911020526
44116CB00026B/32